Vegan Christmas FEASTS

Vegan Christmas FEASTS

Inspired meat-free recipes for the festive season

JACKIE KEARNEY

photography by CLARE WINFIELD

RYLAND PETERS & SMALL

LONDON • NEW YORK

Senior Designer Megan Smith
Design Assistance Emily Breen
Editor Miriam Catley
Production Controller Mai-Ling Collyer
Art Director Leslie Harrington
Editorial Director Julia Charles
Publisher Cindy Richards
Food Stylists Emily Kydd, Katy Gilhooly
    and Jackie Kearney
Prop Stylist Tony Hutchinson
Indexer Vanessa Bird

First published in 2019
by Ryland Peters & Small
20–21 Jockey's Fields,
London WC1R 4BW
and
341 E 116th Street, New York, 10029
www.rylandpeters.com

10 9 8 7 6 5 4 3 2 1

Some of the recipes in this book have been
previously published by Ryland Peters & Small.

Text © Jackie Kearney 2019
Design and photographs
© Ryland Peters & Small 2019

UK ISBN: 978-1-78879-177-9
US ISBN: 978-1-78879-145-8

Printed and bound in China

A CIP record for this book is available from the
British Library.

Notes
· Both British (Metric) and American (Imperial
plus US cups) measurements are included in
these recipes for your convenience, however it is
important to work with one set of measurements
and not alternate between the two within a recipe.
· All spoon measurements are level, unless
otherwise specified.
· Ovens should be preheated to the specified
temperature. Recipes in this book were tested
using a regular oven. If using a fan-assisted/
convection oven, follow the manufacturer's
instructions for adjusting temperatures.
· When a recipe calls for the grated zest of citrus
fruit, buy unwaxed fruit and wash well before use.
If you can only find treated fruit, scrub well in
warm soapy water and rinse before using.

CONTENTS

Festive FEASTS

The holiday season means so many different things to different people. From a turkey at Thanksgiving to a Christmas dinner with all the trimmings, many celebratory feasts traditionally focus on meat. And the feasts in my extended family were no exception. As a young vegetarian, this could be quite challenging. Back then, a plate that excluded meat was often just a selection of rather plain vegetables. Then one year I acquired a new vegetarian cookery book. Linda McCartney's first cookbook was a game-changer for me. And when I discovered there was a recipe for a celebration roast, I was so overjoyed, I made one for my family and one for my best friend who was also vegetarian. I've revisited the recipe for this collection as it remains a very easy dish to prepare and can hold it's own amongst some of the more complex mock meat dishes in this book.

My young family and I have alternated many of our festive holidays between traditional celebrations with our families in the UK and our own adventures in more tropical climes. Over the years we've enjoyed Indian thali, Thai and Burmese banquets for our festive feasts.

The best Christmas breakfast I ever enjoyed was noodle soup on the beach in Koh Ranong, where the odd glittery bauble hanging from a palm tree was the only reminder of the time of year. My children would probably remember their time in Goa at Christmas. As a Christian state there were many local celebrations and our favourite little café, The Cheeky Chapati,

organised a huge vegetarian roast dinner with all the trimmings. Needless to say, there wasn't a spare seat in the place on Christmas Day.

Mixing up the traditional with more exotic flavours opens up a greater variety of feasting dishes. This collection of recipes draws on both my love of home-cooked family celebration dinners, together with some of my favourite party platters and street food gems for sharing. Some of the recipes have been drawn from across my previous recipe collections plus some new festive specials, sweet treats and ideas for making the most of your leftovers.

When I'm at home and cooking for my family and friends, like many home cooks, I spend several days preparing for the upcoming feast, so I've included ideas and tips for dishes that are good to prep ahead. The years of enduring boring plates of plain veggies are long gone and I love surprising people with a large array of mouth-watering vegetable dishes. These so-called sides are often equally as popular as the main event. In recent years, the range and availability of plant-based roasts has hugely expanded, and it's very easy to buy something to substitute for meat. But I find these ready-made versions are quite expensive and often small in size. There's something very lovely about having plant-based showstoppers on the table and it definitely encourages more people to try the plant-based alternatives. Of course food made from scratch always tastes better, too.

SMALL **PLATES**
& SEASONAL
SHARING PLATTERS

AUBERGINE JEOW WARM SALAD

This warm salad combines a classic Laos-style dip with fresh crunchy vegetables, to create a delicious starter or sharing platter perfect for feasting. Jeow refers to the roasted chilli/chile dip, sometimes combining aubergines/eggplants or tomatoes. This spicy and fragrant dip can be served as a blini or crostini topping too (see page 132).

FOR THE JEOW

2 medium-large aubergines/
    eggplants or 8–9 long thin ones
8 large garlic cloves, skin on
2 banana shallots, skin on
3–8 small fresh red chillies/chiles
    (to taste)
1–2½ tablespoons soy sauce
2 tablespoons freshly chopped
    coriander/cilantro
1 tablespoon freshly chopped
    mint leaves

FOR THE SALAD

½ Chinese lettuce, thinly sliced
½ red onion, finely diced
1 red (bell) pepper, deseeded and
    sliced into batons 3 cm x 5 mm/
    1¼ x ¼ inches
large handful of tofu puffs,
    quartered, or fried tempeh pieces
    (optional)
freshly squeezed juice of 1 lime
1 large fresh red chilli/chile,
    to garnish (optional)
large handful of fresh coriander/
    cilantro and mint leaves, torn
handful of toasted peanuts or
    cashew nuts, roughly chopped
    (optional)

baking sheet, lightly oiled

SERVES 4

Preheat the oven to 220°C (425°F) Gas 7.

To make the jeow, pierce the aubergines/eggplants a few times, then place on a non-stick baking sheet and bake in the preheated oven for approximately 30 minutes until the skin is starting to blacken and the aubergines/eggplants are completely soft. Set aside.

Put the garlic cloves, shallots and chillies/chiles onto the prepared baking sheet and roast in the preheated oven for 15–25 minutes until they are also starting to blacken on the outside. They will cook at different times, so keep an eye on them and take them out before they burn.

Once all the vegetables have cooled, remove the tops and skins from each, apart from the chillies/chiles, which only need the tops removing.

Pound all the cooked vegetables together with a pestle and mortar or fork until it reaches a smooth, dip-like consistency. Add 1–2 tablespoons of the soy sauce. Adjust to taste and add more sauce if desired.

If preparing ahead of time, this mixture can be refrigerated for several days and then the remaining steps completed on the day.

Add the chopped herbs to the aubergine/eggplant mixture and mix well. To make the salad, put the lettuce and red onion in a large bowl.

When you are ready to serve, in a small wok or frying pan/skillet, add the red (bell) pepper and stir-fry over a very high heat for a minute, then add the jeow and tofu/tempeh pieces (if using) and stir-fry vigorously for a further minute or two. Remove from the heat and tip into the salad bowl, add the lime juice and mix everything well.

Pile the warm salad high on the serving platter, garnish with the roasted and fresh chillies/chiles and torn herbs and sprinkle with the toasted peanuts or cashew nuts, if using. Serve immediately.

STICKY BBQ TOFU SKEWERS
WITH CUCUMBER & PEANUT DIPPING SAUCE

One of my favourite celebrations in Thailand is the King's birthday on December 5th, when thousands of people take to the streets with their little candles. We ate some incredible street food that night, wandering around the Thieves Market in Thailand, including the most memorable skewer of sticky, spicy barbecued tofu. These divine skewers, served with crunchy cucumber and peanut dipping sauce, befit any celebration.

6 large fresh red chillies/
   chiles
6 garlic cloves, finely
   chopped
2.5-cm/1-inch piece of
   fresh ginger, peeled
   and finely chopped
½ teaspoon ground
   white pepper
2 tablespoons cooking
   sherry or Shaoxing
2 tablespoons vegan fish
   sauce (see page 139,
   optional)
2 tablespoons dark soy
   sauce
4 tablespoons agave syrup
1 tablespoon soft brown
   sugar
½ bunch of fresh
   coriander/cilantro,
   chopped
36 tofu puffs
sea salt
Cucumber & Peanut
   Dipping Sauce to serve
   (optional) and Vegan
   Nam Prik Pao (see
   page 139)

FOR THE CUCUMBER &
PEANUT DIPPING SAUCE
½ cucumber, halved
   lengthways
1 teaspoon light soy
   sauce
3 tablespoons freshly
   squeezed lime juice
2–3 teaspoons soft brown
   sugar, to taste
1 tablespoon peanuts
2 tablespoons rice
   vinegar
1 red shallot, finely
   chopped
1 fresh red and 1 fresh
   green chilli/chile,
   finely chopped
a pinch of sea salt

12 bamboo skewers,
   soaked in cold water
   for 30 minutes
baking sheet, lightly
   greased

SERVES 4–6

To make the dipping sauce, scrape the seeds out from the centre of the cucumber, then thinly slice the flesh into crescents. Put the soy sauce in a bowl, add the lime juice and sugar and stir together until dissolved. Dry-roast the peanuts in a small frying pan/skillet over a medium heat for 4–5 minutes, stirring occasionally, until starting to brown. Leave to cool. Using a pestle and mortar, crush the peanuts to a rough, chunky powder. Add the powder and all the remaining ingredients to the soy sauce mixture and stir well, before pouring over the cucumber and tossing to coat in the dressing. Set aside in the fridge.

In a large bowl, combine the chillies/chiles and all the remaining ingredients, except the tofu puffs. Mix well until all the sugar has dissolved. Check the seasoning and add salt to taste.

Add the tofu puffs to the bowl and stir to coat in the marinade. Cover and set aside in the fridge for at least 1 hour or preferably overnight.

Preheat the grill/broiler to high. Skewer three tofu puffs onto each bamboo skewer. Lay the skewers on the baking sheet and put under the grill/broiler. Grill/broil, turning occasionally, for 10–12 minutes or until golden brown and crispy on the outside. Serve two or three skewers per person with a little pot of the cucumber and peanut dipping sauce and some vegan nam prik pao alongside each portion.

RAINBOW CHARD TARTLETS
WITH BROAD BEAN PURÉE

This is a great vegan alternative to miniature quiches using nutritious gram/chickpea flour, and you can incorporate whatever seasonal vegetables you like. Rainbow chard provides a colourful alternative to spinach, and you can substitute the broad beans for peas, if you like. The tarts can be frozen after baking and can be served warm or cold as a starter or sharing platter. The purée also makes a pretty bruschetta or canapé topping.

1 x 320 g/11½ oz. ready-rolled
   shortcrust pastry, 35 x 23 cm/
   14 x 9 inches
flour, for dusting
120 g/4½ oz. gram/chickpea flour
½ teaspoon black salt (or use any)
½ teaspoon turmeric powder
   (optional)
½ teaspoon salt
½ teaspoon baking powder
120 g/1 cup frozen baby broad beans,
   or substitute frozen peas
½ teaspoon stock powder
½ teaspoon mint sauce
6–7 medium-sized stems of rainbow
   chard, trimmed and chopped into
   3–4-cm/1¼–1½-inch pieces
a handful of freshly chopped thyme
a handful of vegan bacon crispy bits,
   such as Schwartz or McCormicks
   (optional)

8-cm/3¼-inch cookie cutter (or 5-cm/
   2-inch cookie cutter for mini tartlets)
a non-stick 12-hole muffin pan (or a 24-
   hole mini muffin pan), lightly greased

MAKES 12 TARTLETS
(OR 24 MINI TARTLETS)

Preheat the oven to 180°C (350°F) Gas 4.

Lay or roll out the pastry on a well-floured surface. Using an 8-cm/ 3¼-inch cookie cutter (or 5-cm/2-inch cutter for mini tartlets), cut out 12 (or 24) circles. Press the pastry gently into the holes of the prepared muffin pan making sure of a snug fit. Put the pan in the preheated oven for 10–15 minutes until the pastry has started to cook.

Sift the gram/chickpea flour into a large bowl and add the black salt, turmeric powder (if using), salt, 380 ml/13 fl oz. water and baking powder. Whisk to make a smooth batter. Set aside.

Put the broad beans, stock powder and 100 ml/⅓ cup plus 1 tablespoon of water into a small pan and bring to a simmer over a medium heat for a few minutes. Add a little more water if needed, so that there is approximately 2 tablespoons of liquid in the pan after cooking. Remove from the heat, add the mint sauce and blend to a smooth, thick purée. Set aside to cool. This mixture can be frozen or made several days in advance and kept in the fridge.

Put the chard into a small pan and heat gently over a medium heat until it is just wilted, or microwave for 30 seconds to wilt quickly. Put the wilted chard onto paper towels to remove any excess water.

Remove the muffin pan from the oven. Put a small spoonful of wilted chard into the pastry cases and then pour over the batter until each pastry case is almost filled. Carefully put the muffin pan back into the oven and bake for a further 30–40 minutes until the pastry is just golden and the filling is firm. Remove from the oven. The tartlets can be served warm or set aside on a wire rack to cool.

When ready to serve, the tartlets can be gently reheated in a low oven if you like, then pipe or spoon a small swirl of the broad bean purée on top of each tartlet. Decorate with a light scattering of chopped thyme and some vegan bacon crispy bits if you like.

SOM TAM RICE PAPER ROLLS
THAI GREEN PAPAYA SALAD ROLLS

I made this dish for the critic's menu during MasterChef 2011. It's up to you to adjust the amount of chilli/chile you want to use. I like it authentically super-hot which balances against the sweet and salty flavours, but use fewer chillies/chiles (and perhaps a little more sugar) if you want something with less heat, especially if cooking for a crowd. You can always add a chilli/chile dip on the side.

150 g/heaped 1 cup unsalted peanuts
2–8 fresh red bird's-eye chillies/
   chiles, to taste, thinly sliced
6 garlic cloves, peeled and left whole
1 green papaya, peeled, deseeded
   and grated
1 small carrot, grated
a large handful of green beans,
   trimmed and cut into 2.5-cm/
   1-inch pieces
10 cherry tomatoes, quartered
3 tablespoons vegan fish sauce
   (see page 139), vegan
   Worcestershire sauce or light
   soy sauce
3 tablespoons light soy sauce
freshly squeezed juice of 2 limes
3 tablespoons grated palm sugar/
   jaggery
12 sheets of Vietnamese rice paper
a handful of fresh coriander/cilantro
   or basil leaves and/or edible
   flowers, to garnish (optional)

SERVES 4

Preheat the oven to 200°C (400°F) Gas 6.

Scatter the peanuts onto a baking sheet and put in the preheated oven for 8–10 minutes until the peanuts are golden brown and well roasted. Set aside.

Put the chillies/chiles and garlic in a large mortar and grind with a pestle to make a paste. Set the paste aside in a small bowl.

Put the papaya, carrot and green beans in the mortar, and pound gently. Add the cherry tomatoes and pound again for a few minutes until well bruised. Add the vegan fish sauce, soy sauce, lime juice and sugar, and continue to pound until all the ingredients are well mixed. Stir in the chilli/chile and garlic paste.

Set up a large bowl of hot water next to the chopping board. Soak each rice paper sheet for 2–3 minutes in hot water or according to the packet instructions just prior to filling and rolling as follows. Soak the paper until soft, then lay it on a clean dish towel and pat it dry with paper towels. Put it onto the chopping board and put about a twelfth of the papaya mixture in the centre, leaving a 3-cm/1¼-inch border all the way round. Fold in the sides, then roll the paper tightly to create a cigar shape. Repeat with the remaining sheets of rice paper and papaya mixture. Slice the rolls in half at an angle. Serve six halves per person. Garnish with the herbs and/or edible flowers, if you like.

GOURD & CASHEW KOFTAS

These little kofta balls make a great sharing platter for a buffet or family feast and the bejewelled pomegranate raita makes an eye-catching addition to this dish. I use the bottle gourd (from an Pakistani grocers) which looks like a light-green elongated squash. But you could substitute courgette/zucchini or carrot if you like.

FOR THE RAITA

500 g/heaped 2 cups natural/plain
　soya/soy yogurt
a bunch of fresh mint leaves,
　finely chopped
½ teaspoon mint sauce
pomegranate seeds, to serve

MAKES 500 ML/2 CUPS

FOR THE KOFTAS

120 g/1 cup cashew nuts
2 bottle/doodhi gourds, peeled
　and grated
375 g/3 cups gram/chickpea flour
2 large fresh red chillies/chiles,
　finely chopped
1 teaspoon ginger paste
1 teaspoon garlic paste
a large handful of fresh coriander/
　cilantro
1 teaspoon chaat masala
1 teaspoon salt, or to taste
vegetable oil, for shallow-frying

SERVES 4–6

To make the raita, put the yogurt in a small bowl and add the mint and mint sauce. Stir well to combine. (Alternatively, you can blitz the unchopped mint with a stick blender and a few tablespoons of the yogurt, then mix this with the remaining yogurt. Don't use a blender on all the yogurt, though, because it breaks down the thickness of the yogurt and becomes too liquid.) Stir in the pomegranate seeds. Set aside.

For the koftas, toast the cashew nuts in a dry frying pan/skillet over a medium heat for 1–2 minutes, stirring occasionally, until golden. Set aside. Put the grated gourds into a colander and drain the excess liquid, squeezing the grated flesh to remove as much water as possible. Put the flour into a bowl and add the chillies/chiles, cashews, ginger and garlic pastes, fresh coriander/cilantro, chaat masala and salt. Add 240–360 ml/1–1½ cups of water to form a thick paste. Taste the paste and add more salt if necessary.

Half-fill a frying pan/skillet with vegetable oil and place over a medium heat. Test the oil temperature by dropping a little batter into the oil, when it rises to the top and sizzles without burning, the oil is ready for frying. Wet your hands and form the koftas mixture into 16–18 loose balls, each about the size of a golf ball. Gently drop the koftas into the hot oil (do not overcrowd the pan) and fry in batches until golden brown and cooked through (approximately 6–8 minutes). Drain on paper towels and serve with the raita.

SWEET-&-SOUR POPCORN TOFU

For an impressive appetizer or sharing platter, put a little sauce in a Chinese soup spoon and top with a piece of tofu. In my quest to give tofu texture and flavour, there are quite a lot of processes involved, but you can save time by using a ready-made plum sauce, if you like.

6 tablespoons light soy sauce

2 teaspoons Chinese five-spice powder

400 g/14 oz. firm tofu, cut into bite-sized pieces

150 g/1 cup cornflour/cornstarch

100 ml/⅓ cup plus 1 tablespoon soya/soy cream

150 g/2¾ cups panko breadcrumbs

1 teaspoon hot smoked paprika

vegetable oil, for deep-frying

steamed rice (optional), to serve

FOR THE PLUM SAUCE

12 plums, stoned/pitted and roughly chopped

4–6 tablespoons soft brown sugar

8 tablespoons rice vinegar, or to taste

1 tablespoon tomato purée/paste, or to taste

½ teaspoon salt

SERVES 4–6

To make the plum sauce, put the plums in a pan over a medium heat and add 2 tablespoons of water and the sugar. Bring to the boil, then simmer for 15 minutes or until the fruit is completely softened. Add the remaining sauce ingredients and bring to a simmer again, adding a little water if necessary so that the sauce is not too thick. Using a food processor or blender, blend the sauce until smooth. Check the seasoning and adjust the sugar, salt or vinegar to taste. The balance of sweet-and-sour flavours means one should not overpower the other. Set aside.

Mix the soy sauce and five-spice powder in a small bowl, then drizzle this marinade over the tofu pieces. Put the cornflour/cornstarch in one bowl, the soya/soy cream in another bowl and the panko breadcrumbs in a third bowl. Add the paprika to the panko breadcrumbs and mix well.

Heat 600 ml/2½ cups of vegetable oil in a wok over a medium-high heat. Meanwhile, put a sheet of greaseproof paper on the work surface. Dip each piece of tofu in the cornflour/cornstarch, then in the soya/soy cream and then in the breadcrumbs, shaping it a little to form a ball. Lay each coated ball on the greaseproof paper as you go.

Deep-fry the tofu balls in batches, until golden brown and crispy. Lift out using a slotted spoon and drain on paper towels. You can keep the tofu balls warm in a low oven at 140°C (275°F) Gas 1, if you like, or reheat them later at 180°C (350°F) Gas 4 for 10–15 minutes. Serve with the plum sauce.

BEETROOT & WATERCRESS SAMOSAS
WITH QUICK PINEAPPLE CHUTNEY

India's ubiquitous street food, the samosa, transfers seamlessly to the festive party scene. These crispy filled pockets are the perfect light bite. If you don't have a spice grinder to make the whole spice mix or are short on time, then you can just substitute some garam masala powder. You can buy whole cooked beetroots/beets to save time, too, but make sure they haven't been pickled. If you buy whole beetroots/beets with the leaves, then you can also chop the leaves and add them to the filling along with the watercress. I like to eat these samosas with a simple spicy pineapple and nigella seed chutney. It is the perfect combination of the plentiful (beetroot/beet) and the exotic (pineapple). It sounds a little different, but I promise you the flavours will make your mouth sing.

FOR THE PASTRY
240 g/1¾ cups plain/
    all-purpose flour
1 teaspoon ajwain (carom)
    seeds
4 tablespoons vegetable
    oil
1 teaspoon sea salt

FOR THE FILLING
1 teaspoon cumin seeds
1 clove
4 black peppercorns
2 green cardamom pods
½ teaspoon fennel seeds
1 teaspoon coriander
    seeds
1 tablespoon coconut
    or vegetable oil
5–7.5-cm/2–3-inch piece
    of fresh ginger, finely
    chopped
1–2 fresh green chillies/
    chiles, to taste, finely
    chopped
1 teaspoon mild chilli/
    chili powder

1 teaspoon amchoor
    (green mango powder)
pinch of asafoetida
    powder (hing)
2–3 large beetroots/beets,
    boiled, peeled, cut into
    1-cm/½-inch cubes
bunch of watercress,
    roughly chopped
½ teaspoon salt, to taste
1 litre/quart vegetable oil,
    for deep-frying

MAKES 12–16

FOR THE QUICK
PINEAPPLE CHUTNEY
90 g/scant ½ cup
    granulated sugar
150 ml/⅔ cup rice vinegar
2 teaspoons nigella seeds
1 fresh red chilli/chile,
    finely chopped
1 medium pineapple,
    peeled, cored and
    diced into 1.5-cm/
    ½-inch pieces

MAKES 500 ML/2 CUPS

For the chutney, add the sugar and rice vinegar to a medium pan and place over a low-medium heat. Bring to a simmer, dissolving all the sugar, then add the nigella seeds and chilli/chile. Stir well and cook for a few minutes. Remove from the heat, add the pineapple pieces and mix well. Set aside to cool, then spoon into sterilized jars, seal and keep in the fridge (it keeps for up to 1 week).

To make the pastry, mix together the flour, ajwain (carom) seeds, oil and salt. Rub together to create a crumb consistency. Add 6 tablespoons of water gradually, kneading together until you get a soft dough. Cover with a damp kitchen towel and leave to rest for 30 minutes.

Next, make the filling. Set aside ½ teaspoon of the cumin seeds to use later in the filling, then toast the rest of the whole spices for the samosas in a pan and then grind them to a fine powder using a pestle and mortar.

Heat the oil in a large frying pan/skillet or wok and add the ginger and green chillies/chiles. Cook gently for about 2–3 minutes, then add the reserved whole cumin seeds, and cook for another 1–2 minutes until they start to crackle.

Add the freshly ground spice mix (or use 2 teaspoons garam masala) and then the chilli/chili powder, amchoor, asafoetida and beetroot/beet cubes. Mix well and cook gently for 3–4 minutes. Remove from the heat and add the watercress and salt to taste. Mix well and set aside to cool.

Knead the dough and divide into 6–8 equal balls. Lightly dust the work surface with flour and roll out the balls into large discs.

Cut each circle of pastry in half down the middle and take one half of the pastry circle into your hand. Brush some water down the straight edge and bring together those edges, like a cone, and seal them well.

Fill the cone of pastry with about a tablespoonful of filling, then dampen the edge and seal closed by pinching the top edges together. Repeat with the remaining dough to make 12–16 samosas (depending on how big you want to make them).

To fry the samosas, heat the vegetable oil for deep-frying in a deep pan. Drop a cube of bread into the oil to check that the oil is hot enough; it should sizzle immediately and rise to the surface.

Gently deep-fry your samosas, in batches until lightly browned, for about 8 minutes, turning halfway through. Drain the samosas on paper towels, then keep them warm in a low oven while you cook the remaining batches. Alternatively, allow them to cool and then reheat later. They will keep in the fridge for several days. Serve with the pineapple chutney.

CHESTNUT & PORCINI CREAM MILLE-FEUILLE

These delicate appetizers are a little fiddly to prepare but totally worth the effort. You can prepare the pastry layers and filling in advance, as both freeze well. The pastry layers will benefit from another flash in a warm oven to ensure they are crispy, but make sure they are cooled before putting together. Then simply construct the mille-feuille just before serving.

40 g/1½ oz. dried porcini mushrooms, or substitute any dried wild mushrooms (makes 100 g/3½ oz. rehydrated)
250 ml/1 cup plus 1 tablespoon boiling water
1 x 320 g/11½ oz. ready-rolled puff pastry sheet or block (rolled out to approx. 38 x 22 cm /15 x 8½ inches)
3 tablespoons olive oil
2 red onions, thinly sliced
2 tablespoons balsamic or red wine vinegar
2 tablespoons soft brown sugar

1 teaspoon fine sea salt
1 teaspoon ground white pepper
18 ready-roasted chestnuts, roughly chopped (approx. 5 mm/¼ inch pieces)
1 x 200 ml/7 fl. oz. tub of Oatly crème fraîche, or other vegan thickened cream
3 tablespoons freshly chopped parsley (or substitute 2 teaspoons dried)
2 tablespoons freshly chopped thyme (or substitute 1 teaspoon dried)

MAKES 8–10

Soak the dried mushrooms in the boiling water, ensuring that they are well covered. Set aside for 15 minutes.

Preheat the oven to 200°C (400°F) Gas 6.

If using ready-rolled pastry, leave the greaseproof sheet on one side as you unroll. If using a block, cut a piece of baking paper into a large rectangle and lightly brush with oil. Place the block of puff pastry in the middle of the sheet and, using a rolling pin dusted with flour, roll out the pastry until it's approximately 5 mm/¼ inch thick, and 38 x 22 cm/ 15 x 8½ inches in size. It doesn't matter if it goes over the edges of the baking sheet as it will shrink back when cooking. Trim the edges with a sharp knife and then carefully cut the pastry into identical rectangles (approx. 16–20 depending on shrinkage), each approximately 9 x 4 cm/3½ x 1½ inches. Try not to cut through the paper.

Lift the pastry together with the greaseproof baking paper onto a large baking sheet. Brush the top of the pastry with a little olive oil. Prick the pastry all over with a fork and place a second baking sheet on

top. This will help keep a nice even shape and stop it rising too much. Bake the pastry in the preheated for 20–25 minutes, or according to packet instructions until golden brown and crisp.

Take the baking sheets out of the oven and leave to cool for 5 minutes before removing the top baking sheet. Let cool completely.

In a small frying pan/skillet, add the remaining tablespoon of olive oil and the sliced onions. Fry over a low heat for 15 minutes until starting to brown then add the vinegar and brown sugar. Cook for a further 15–20 minutes until the onions are sticky and soft. Season with ¼ teaspoon of the salt and the white pepper. Set aside to cool.

Carefully remove the mushrooms from the water. The sediment will settle at the bottom of the bowl, so removing mushrooms carefully will avoid transferring any gritty bits. Keep the liquid and carefully pour through a tea strainer into a small pan and place over a high heat. Bring the liquid to a simmer and reduce to approximately 1–2 tablespoons of thickened liquid. Set aside to cool.

Pat dry the mushrooms with some paper towels then roughly chop and set aside.

In a blender, add a quarter of the chestnuts, the reduced mushroom liquid, ½ teaspoon salt and the Oatly crème fraîche. Blend to make a thick cream. Pour into a bowl and add the chopped mushrooms and the remaining chestnuts. Add the herbs (holding back a spoonful for garnishing) and mix well.

Carefully separate the pastry rectangles each into two halves. This will give you approximately 32–40 rectangles (depending on breakages) with the aim of making 8–10 portions.

To construct each mille-feuille, place the bottom layer of pastry on a plate and add a heaped dessertspoonful of the mushroom chestnut mixture. Place a pastry layer on top then gently spoon a layer of red onion mixture on top and spread gently. Place another pastry layer on top and then spoon more mushroom-chestnut mixture on top. Add another pastry slice, so that each mille-feuille will have four pastry layers. Repeat with the rest of the pastry slices and filling. Sprinkle the remaining herbs on top to garnish.

Serve immediately on a sharing platter or as a starter with a simple green salad.

CAULIFLOWER & KALE PAKORAS

Pakoras are easy to adapt to include whichever seasonal vegetables you have available. Cauliflower and kale is one of my favourite combinations, because the kale adds extra crispness. I always make a big batch, as they keep well in the fridge or even freezer, and can easily be reheated in the oven. Serve with raita (see page 18) or mango chutney.

1 small cauliflower, cut into 2-cm/¾-inch florets

1 tablespoon sunflower oil, plus extra for deep-frying

2 onions, thinly sliced

a bunch of kale or dark leaf cabbage, thinly sliced

2–4 small fresh green chillies/chiles, to taste, finely chopped

2 large fresh red chillies/chiles, finely chopped

1 tablespoon chilli/chili powder

½ teaspoon asafoetida powder

250 g/2 cups gram/chickpea flour

2 teaspoons black cumin seeds

2 tablespoons fennel seeds

2 tablespoons dried pomegranate seeds (anardana)

a bunch of fresh coriander/cilantro, roughly chopped

¼ teaspoon bicarbonate of soda/baking soda

1 teaspoon salt

raita (see page 18), to serve

MAKES ABOUT 24

FOR THE DANIYA

2 bunches of fresh coriander/cilantro

a bunch of fresh mint leaves

200 ml/scant 1 cup coconut milk

4–8 small fresh green chillies/chiles, trimmed

freshly squeezed juice of ½ lemon

½ tablespoon caster/superfine sugar

¼ onion

¼ teaspoon salt

MAKES ABOUT 400 ML/1¾ CUPS

To make the daniya, put all the ingredients in a food processor or blender and process until smooth. Taste and adjust the seasoning with salt as needed. Cover and store in the fridge for up to 1 week until needed.

Parboil the cauliflower for 2–3 minutes, then drain in a colander and leave for 5 minutes.

Heat the oil in a small pan over a medium heat and fry the onions for 5 minutes or until softened. Add the kale or cabbage, green and red chillies/chiles, chilli/chili powder and asafoetida, and cook for 3 minutes. Set aside.

Sift the gram/chickpea flour into a large bowl. Toast the cumin and fennel seeds in a dry pan over a medium heat for 30 seconds, stirring occasionally, to release the aroma, then add to the gram/chickpea flour followed by the onion and kale mixture. Add 120 ml/scant ½ cup of water to make a thick paste, then add all the other ingredients and mix well. The batter should have a thick porridge-like consistency, so add a little more gram/chickpea flour or water if necessary.

Heat the oil for deep-frying in a deep pan until hot. Using a tablespoon, gently drop spoonfuls of the pakora mixture into the hot oil, frying in batches of three or four. Fry for 6–8 minutes until sizzling subsides and the pakoras are golden and crispy, turning halfway through to cook both sides. Remove with a slotted spoon and drain on paper towels. Deep fry the rest in the same way. Put the cooked pakoras in a low oven until ready to serve. Serve hot, with some daniya and raita.

SHIITAKE MUSHROOM CROQUETAS

This vegan twist on a classic Spanish comfort dish will win over the most sceptical of guests, with the crispy exterior giving way to a rich, creamy centre, they're always a crowdpleaser at any party. Croquetas traditionally have a thick béchamel filling, which is often spiked with Spain's favourite hammy surprise. You could use vegan 'lardons' or substitute other vegetables for the mushrooms if you like. Dried porcini make a good substitute for shiitake in this recipe.

4 tablespoons olive oil

1 baby leek, thinly sliced

2 bay leaves

½ teaspoon rock salt

4 tablespoons plain/all-purpose flour

500 ml/2 cups plus 2 tablespoons almond milk

3–4 dried shiitake mushrooms, soaked in boiling water for 15 minutes, drained

1 flax 'egg' (see page 138) or egg replacer

80 g/2 cups panko breadcrumbs

2 tablespoons nutritional yeast

½ teaspoon fine salt

½ teaspoon freshly ground white pepper

vegetable oil, for deep-frying

1 tablespoon grated vegan Italian-style hard cheese, to serve (optional)

MAKES 10–12

To make the filling, heat 2 tablespoons of the olive oil in a frying pan/skillet over a medium heat. Add the leek and sauté until softened. Add the bay leaves, salt and flour and stir well. Cook the flour mixture for about 3–4 minutes, and then slowly add the milk. Mix well to make a smooth paste. Keep cooking the flour mixture over a gentle heat for about 10–15 minutes until well thickened, like mashed potato.

In a separate small pan, add the remaining 2 tablespoons of olive oil and place over a high heat. Chop the drained shiitake mushrooms into cubes and fry in the oil until slightly crisped. Set aside on paper towels.

Put the flax 'egg' mixture in a small bowl and mix the panko breadcrumbs, nutritional yeast, salt and pepper in another small bowl.

When the filling mixture has cooled, use your hands to shape it into 10–12 balls. Dip each ball into the 'egg' mixture then into the panko mixture. Set aside on a tray ready to fry.

Preheat the oven to 120°C (250°F) Gas ½.

Heat the olive oil for deep-frying in a deep pan over a medium-high heat. When the oil is ready, it should just sizzle when you drop a little breadcrumb mixture into the pan. Fry the croquetas, in small batches of 5 or 6, for about 6–8 minutes until golden brown all over. Drain on paper towels and keep warm in the oven until ready to serve. Sprinkle with the vegan Italian-style hard cheese, if you like. Serve at once, if they make it to the table!

HEART OF PALM 'CALAMARI'
WITH GARLIC AIOLI

This recipe has appeared elsewhere within other much longer recipes as an optional addition. Hardly fair for a recipe that makes an impressive appetizer or sharing platter! You can flavour the batter with whatever spicing you like. I favour Korean red pepper flakes or powder or just use dried chilli/chili flakes, but you can also keep this plain and simple served with nothing more than lemon wedges.

FOR THE 'CALAMARI' RINGS
200 g/7 oz. can heart of palm 'rings'
1 tablespoon rice flour
1 tablespoon potato flour
1 tablespoon plain/all-purpose flour
½ teaspoon sea salt
2 tablespoons Korean red pepper flakes or powder
150–250 ml/⅔–1 cup plus 1 tablespoon sparkling water
300–400 ml/1¼–scant 1¾ cups vegetable oil, for deep-frying, such as sunflower or rapeseed oil
lemon wedge, to serve

FOR THE AIOLI
6 tablespoons vegan mayonnaise
½ tablespoon freshly squeezed lemon juice
1 small garlic clove, finely chopped
¼ teaspoon sea salt
¼ teaspoon freshly ground white pepper

SERVES 3–4

To make the aioli, mix together all the ingredients in a small bowl. Set aside.

To make the 'calamari' rings, rinse the heart of palm rings and drain on paper towels. Slice into 2.5-cm/1-inch rounds. Carefully push out the centre of each ring with your fingertip (this flaky part of the palm is perfect for making the ravioli filling on page 60). Repeat with the other rounds.

Mix the rice, potato and plain/all-purpose flour together in a small bowl, add the salt and Korean red pepper flakes or powder. Add 150 ml/⅔ cup of the sparkling water and mix well to form a runny batter that should coat the back of a spoon. Add more sparkling water, if needed.

Preheat the oven to 120°C (250°F) Gas ½.

Heat the oil for deep-frying in a small frying pan/skillet until approximately 190°C/375°F. Check the oil temperature with a small drop of batter, it should sizzle but not burn. Dip the heart of palm rings into the batter to coat and then carefully drop into the hot oil, frying in batches of six or seven for 2–3 minutes until the batter is golden and crispy. Drain on paper towels. Put the cooked rings in the low oven to keep warm whilst frying the remaining batches. Serve immediately with lemon wedges and the aioli dip.

HOISIN MOCK DUCK & CHILLI-BEAN TOFU LETTUCE CUPS
WITH STEAMED FLOWER BUNS

Little Gem/Bibb lettuce cups make a fantastic basis for a sharing platter, and you can top them with so many different fillings. The mock duck filling is very easy to prepare and makes a delicious sweet and tangy contrast to the chilli/chile-bean tofu filling. Chilli/chile bean paste (called doubanjiang or Toban djan) is very spicy and made with fermented soy and broad beans. The fillings can be prepared well in advance as they keep for several days in the fridge.

2 Little Gem/Bibb or mini Romaine lettuces

100-g/3½-oz. packet of preserved mustard greens (optional), to serve

FOR THE STEAMED BUNS

½ teaspoon white sugar

½ tablespoon easy-blend active dried yeast

250 g/2 cups plain/all-purpose flour, plus extra to dust

a splash of groundnut/peanut oil, plus extra to grease

1 tablespoon sea salt flakes (use black or coloured if you can find them)

1 tablespoon Sichuan peppercorns, lightly crushed

FOR THE CHILLI/CHILE-BEAN FILLING

2 tablespoons groundnut/peanut or vegetable oil

2 slices mock bacon (optional), chopped into small pieces, or soy-marinated tempeh

400 g/14 oz. firm tofu, rinsed, drained and chopped into 2-cm/¾-inch pieces

1 tablespoon chilli/chile bean paste

1 teaspoon Sichuan sweet bean paste

2 teaspoons fermented black beans

1 teaspoon dark soy sauce

1 teaspoon caster/superfine sugar

6 baby leeks, thinly sliced at an angle

sea salt (optional)

FOR HOISIN SEITAN FILLING

280-g/10-oz. can seitan (mock duck or chicken made from gluten), washed and shredded

4 tablespoons hoisin sauce

½ cucumber

6 spring onions/scallions, cut in half, then thinly sliced lengthways

baking sheet, lightly greased

SERVES 4–6

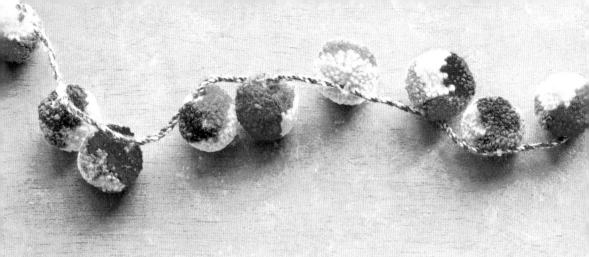

To make the buns, put the sugar and yeast in a bowl and add 125 ml/
½ cup of lukewarm water, then leave in a warm place for 15 minutes
until frothy.

Put the flour into a large bowl and make a well in the centre. Pour
in the yeast mixture, with 2 tablespoons warm water. Mix well to form
a soft dough, then knead the dough vigorously on a floured work surface
for 10 minutes. Put in a well-oiled bowl, cover with a damp dish towel
and leave in a warm place for 2 hours or until the dough has doubled
in size. Lightly knead again to knock out the air. Leave for another
30 minutes.

Put the dough on a floured surface and knead again for a few
minutes. Then roll the dough into a long, wide sausage shape about
20 cm/8 inch wide. Brush the surface with a small amount of oil, then
sprinkle lightly with about 1 teaspoon each of sea salt flakes and Sichuan
peppercorns – just enough of a scatter for a pop of flavour.

Roll up the dough to make a long, thin Swiss roll/jelly roll shape
and pinch each end to seal. Using a sharp knife, cut into 2-cm/¾-inch
slices. Lay the slices on the work surface and, using a pair of chopsticks,
squeeze the opposite sides of each roll together slightly, to make a loose
figure-of-eight. Sprinkle 2 peppercorns and salt flakes onto each.

Put in a lightly oiled steamer and then steam for 10 minutes until
fully risen and cooked. The buns can be kept warm in the steamer until
ready to serve.

For the lettuce cups, trim the ends of the lettuces and gently remove
the whole outer leaves, then set aside for later.

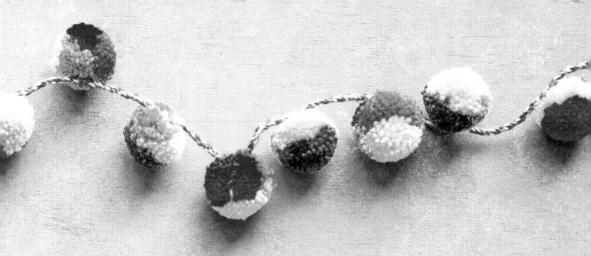

To make the chilli/chile-bean filling, heat 1 tablespoon of the oil in a small frying pan/skillet and cook the mock bacon, if using, until golden brown. Set aside on paper towels. Add another ½ tablespoon of the oil and fry the tofu in batches until crispy and brown on the outside. Set aside on paper towels.

To make the hoisin seitan filling, put the seitan in a small bowl and add 2 tablespoons of the hoisin sauce. Leave to marinate for 20 minutes.

Preheat the oven to 200°C (400°F) Gas 6. Lay the mock duck on the prepared baking sheet in one layer, then bake for 10–15 minutes until the seitan is starting to crisp and tastes chewy.

Using a teaspoon, scrape out the watery seeds from the centre of the cucumber. Cut the flesh into fine matchsticks and set aside.

Heat a wok over a medium heat, add the remaining ½ tablespoon of oil for the chilli/chile-bean filling, then add the chilli/chile bean paste, the sweet bean paste and fermented black beans. Stir-fry for a few minutes, and then add the soy sauce and sugar. Check the seasoning and add salt if necessary, but it shouldn't need it as the black beans are salty.

Add the fried tofu and mock bacon, if using, and cook for 1 minute, then add the baby leeks and cook until the leeks are just softening. Set aside until ready to serve.

To serve, lay four lettuce cups onto each plate, and half-fill two lettuce cups with hoisin seitan filling and two with the chilli/chile-bean filling. Top each of the hoisin seitan lettuce cups with a pinch of sliced spring onions/scallions and cucumber slivers, then drizzle with a little of the remaining hoisin sauce. Add a steamed bun to each serving and serve each with a teaspoon of preserved mustard greens, if you like.

ARTICHOKE TORTA
WITH SAFFRON MAYONNAISE

These Italian-style pies are also hard to resist. Lighter than most British pies, the flaky, crispy pastry with a rich and savoury filling, is served across Italy, and is usually packed with eggs and butter. These pies can be made-ahead and served as a light bite, or alternatively, add polenta chips and aioli for a more hearty dish.

450 g/1 lb. artichoke hearts (approx. 5 fresh artichokes or 1½ small jars)

2 tablespoons pomace or vegetable oil

2 banana shallots, finely chopped

2 garlic cloves, crushed, then chopped

100 g/3½ oz. barely cooked white rice

2 tablespoons fine chickpea/gram flour

1–2 teaspoons salt, to taste

2 tablespoons nutritional yeast

8 filo/phyllo pastry sheets

FOR THE SAFFRON MAYONNAISE

¼ teaspoon saffron threads, soaked for 10 minutes in 2 tablespoons boiling water

5 generous tablespoons vegan mayonnaise (see page 139)

4 small tart pans or shallow pie pans (7.5 cm/3 inch), or 1 large shallow pie pan (25 cm/10 inch), lightly oiled

SERVES 4

First slice the fresh artichoke hearts. If using jarred artichokes, rinse with warm water, drain and dry well before slicing.

Preheat the oven to 180°C (350°F) Gas 4.

Heat ½ tablespoon of the oil in a small frying pan/skillet and sauté the shallots for 6–7 minutes until soft and translucent. Add the garlic and cook for another 2 minutes. Set aside.

Add the prepared artichoke hearts to the shallot and garlic mixture, along with the cooked rice. In a small bowl, mix together the fine chickpea/gram flour with 4–6 tablespoons of water, or enough to make a thick but pourable paste. Add the paste to the artichoke mixture, along with the salt and nutritional yeast.
Mix well to ensure all the ingredients are well combined.

If using individual pans, layer two sheets of filo/phyllo pastry into each pan, offsetting the squares to make a star shape and ensuring the pastry is snugly pushed into the corners. If using a large pie pan, layer your filo/phyllo sheets one at a time, offsetting each sheet to ensure there is at least a double layer of pastry all the way around the pan.

Fill the pastry with the artichoke mixture, until level with the top edge of the pan(s), then fold and twist the pastry across the top, so the filling is covered and the pie(s) is sealed.

Lightly brush the top of the pastry with the remaining oil. Place the pie(s) onto a baking sheet and bake in the preheated oven for about 30–35 minutes until the pastry is golden brown (if baking one large pie, cook for a further 15 minutes).

Strain the saffron water to remove the threads, then whisk the saffron water into the vegan mayonnaise, adding slowly and whisking all the time. Serve the warm pie(s) with a generous spoonful of the saffron mayonnaise. It is also nice with polenta chips and a chopped salad.

CRISPY STUFFED TOFU POCKETS

This popular snack from Indonesia, also found in Malaysia, is a moreish light bite, perfect to serve with drinks at any gathering. Kecap manis is an Indonesian sweet soy sauce that is flavoured with garlic and sometimes star anise. The tofu should be the fresh firm variety that hasn't been frozen, so as to maintain the soft middle with a crispy outside.

vegetable oil, for deep-frying
800 g/1¾ lb. firm tofu, cut into
    8 squares, 6 cm/2½ inches across
1 large cucumber, halved lengthways
100 g/1¾ cups beansprouts
3 tablespoons peanuts

FOR THE SAUCE
2 tablespoons soft brown sugar
1–2 small fresh red chillies/chiles,
    finely chopped
2 tablespoons tamarind water,
    or 1 teaspoon tamarind
    concentrate dissolved in
    2 tablespoons hot water
1 tablespoon vegan fish sauce
    (see page 139), or light soy sauce
    and a pinch of seaweed flakes
3 tablespoons kecap manis
    (Indonesian sweet soy sauce)

SERVES 4–6

Heat the oil for deep-frying in a wok or large pan and deep-fry the tofu pieces in batches for 6–8 minutes until they are golden brown and crispy on the outside. Drain on paper towels and set aside to cool.

Put all the sauce ingredients into a food processor or blender and process to make a thick sauce.

Using a teaspoon, scrape out the seeds from the centre of the cucumber. Slice the flesh thinly at an angle. Bring a large pan of water to the boil. Add the beansprouts and blanch for 30 seconds. Drain, then set aside on paper towels. Toast the peanuts in a dry pan over a medium heat for 1–2 minutes, stirring occasionally, until golden. Chop them, then set aside.

Preheat the grill/broiler. Cut a slit horizontally into the tofu pieces to make a pocket. Brush a little of the sauce onto the outside. Grill/broil for 3 minutes on each side. Drizzle a little sauce inside each tofu pocket, then stuff some beansprouts and cucumber pieces inside, with some sticking out. Drizzle with more sauce, then scatter toasted peanuts on top and serve.

SOUPS &
HEARTY
SUPPERS

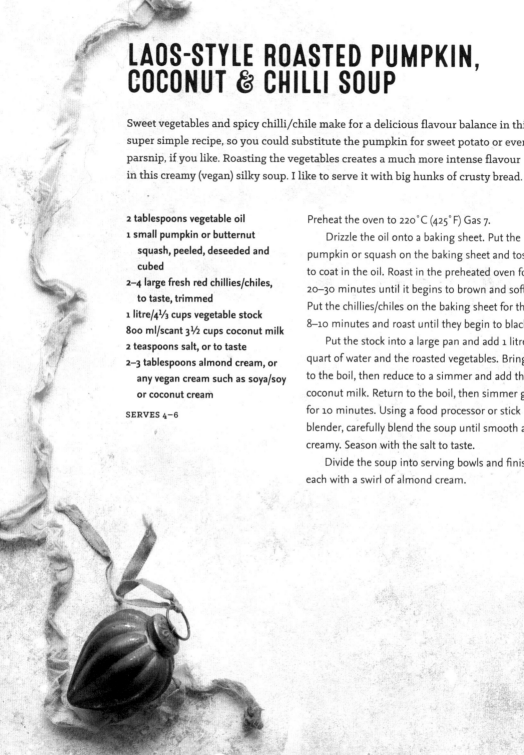

LAOS-STYLE ROASTED PUMPKIN, COCONUT & CHILLI SOUP

Sweet vegetables and spicy chilli/chile make for a delicious flavour balance in this super simple recipe, so you could substitute the pumpkin for sweet potato or even parsnip, if you like. Roasting the vegetables creates a much more intense flavour in this creamy (vegan) silky soup. I like to serve it with big hunks of crusty bread.

2 tablespoons vegetable oil

1 small pumpkin or butternut squash, peeled, deseeded and cubed

2–4 large fresh red chillies/chiles, to taste, trimmed

1 litre/4⅓ cups vegetable stock

800 ml/scant 3½ cups coconut milk

2 teaspoons salt, or to taste

2–3 tablespoons almond cream, or any vegan cream such as soya/soy or coconut cream

SERVES 4–6

Preheat the oven to 220°C (425°F) Gas 7.

Drizzle the oil onto a baking sheet. Put the pumpkin or squash on the baking sheet and toss to coat in the oil. Roast in the preheated oven for 20–30 minutes until it begins to brown and soften. Put the chillies/chiles on the baking sheet for the last 8–10 minutes and roast until they begin to blacken.

Put the stock into a large pan and add 1 litre/ quart of water and the roasted vegetables. Bring to the boil, then reduce to a simmer and add the coconut milk. Return to the boil, then simmer gently for 10 minutes. Using a food processor or stick blender, carefully blend the soup until smooth and creamy. Season with the salt to taste.

Divide the soup into serving bowls and finish each with a swirl of almond cream.

BLASKET BUNNY

CRUSTY SODA BREAD FILLED WITH VEGETABLE & GUINNESS STEW

I created this comforting stew to celebrate one of Ireland's most famous exports, Guinness, becoming a vegan product. Bunny Chow hails from South Africa and is usually a loaf of roll hollowed out and filled with a spiced stew or dhal.

FOR THE SODA BREAD
800 g/6 cups wholemeal/
    whole-wheat flour
1½ teaspoons
    bicarbonate of soda/
    baking soda
1½ teaspoons fine rock
    salt
3 teaspoons freshly
    squeezed lemon juice
750 ml/3¼ cups almond
    milk
handful of coarse
    polenta, for sprinkling

FOR THE STEW
2 tablespoons vegetable
    oil
2 celery sticks, finely
    chopped
4 small white onions,
    2 finely chopped and
    2 sliced
500 g/1 lb. 2 oz. chestnut
    or button mushrooms,
    cleaned and halved
1 tablespoon plain/
    all-purpose flour
600 ml/2½ cups
    Guinness

400 g/14 oz. waxy
    potatoes, peeled and
    cut into 2.5-cm/1-inch
    chunks
2 large carrots, peeled
    and thickly sliced
2 turnips, peeled and
    cut into 2.5-cm/1-inch
    chunks
½ small swede, peeled
    and cut into 2.5-cm/
    1-inch chunks
½ teaspoon mustard
    powder
2 tablespoons dark soy
    sauce
1 teaspoon yeast extract
    or ½ tablespoon
    tomato purée/paste
2 tablespoons good-
    quality vegetable
    bouillon
2 bay leaves
1 sprig of thyme
1–2 teaspoons salt,
    to taste
handful of freshly
    chopped parsley,
    to serve

1 baking sheet, lightly oiled

SERVES 4

Preheat the oven to 200°C (400°F) Gas 6. Add a tablespoon of polenta to the oiled baking sheet and shake it until it is well covered.

To prepare the soda bread, place the flour in a large bowl, add the bicarbonate of/baking soda and salt, then mix well. In a jug/pitcher, combine the lemon juice and almond milk. Pour the liquid into the flour and gently knead together for no more than a minute or two to make a soft dough. Divide the dough into four pieces and roll each to form a small ball. Place on the prepared baking sheet and cut a cross into the top of each ball, about 1 cm/½ inch deep. Bake for 15–20 minutes until the soda bread is lightly browned. Tap the bottom to check the sound is hollow. Set aside to cool.

For the stew, heat the oil in a large, heavy-based pan over a high heat. Add the celery sticks, the two chopped onions and four of the mushrooms, finely chopped. Sauté on a medium heat until dark golden brown and well caramelized.

Add the flour and mix well, cooking gently for 2–3 minutes. Pour in the Guinness and mix well, scraping up any browned bits from the bottom of the pan to make a rich roux. Add all the remaining ingredients and bring to the boil, then simmer, uncovered, for 40–50 minutes until all the vegetables are fully cooked.

Slice the tops off the cooled soda breads and scoop out the middle. Serve the vegetable stew inside the hollowed-out breads and top with the soda breads lid and chopped parsley.

FRENCH ONION SOUP
WITH CASHEW CHEESE CROUTONS

I'm a big soup lover. And after tomato, this is my other childhood favourite. It joined a number of disappointing food moments when I found out there was a bone-based broth to the onions, but I came across vegetarian versions in the Savoie region of the Alps, where tourism has increased the veggie options available.

FOR THE SOUP

3 tablespoons pomace
    or coconut oil
6–8 large Spanish onions,
    thinly sliced
8 garlic cloves, peeled
½ teaspoon freshly
    ground white pepper
½ teaspoon freshly
    ground black pepper
1–2 teaspoons salt,
    to taste
1 teaspoon fresh thyme
    (or ½ teaspoon dried)
2 tablespoons plain/all-
    purpose flour
1.2 litres/5 cups water
350 ml/1½ cups vegan
    red wine
3 bay leaves
1 tablespoon good-
    quality vegetable stock
    powder/bouillon (such
    as Marigold)
1 teaspoon yeast extract
    (or 1 extra tablespoon
    stock powder/bouillon)

FOR THE CASHEW
CHEESE CROUTONS

120 g/1 cup cashews,
    soaked in water for
    3 hours
300 ml/1¼ cups almond
    milk
2 tablespoons tapioca
    flour
4 tablespoons nutritional
    yeast
1 teaspoon garlic powder
½–1 teaspoon salt
½ baguette, cut at an
    angle into thick slices
    and toasted
handful of freshly
    snipped chives, to
    garnish (optional)

SERVES 4

Place a large heavy-based pan over a medium-high heat and add the oil and sliced onions. Sauté the onions for 20 minutes until they are nicely browned and softening. Stir regularly to avoid burning.

Add the garlic, white and black pepper, salt and thyme and cook for a further 5 minutes. Add the flour and cook for another 2 minutes. Add 250–500 ml/1–2 cups of the water and scrape the base of the pan with a wooden spoon to ensure the onions are not sticking and the flour gets well mixed in with the liquid to form a thick paste.

Add the remaining water, the wine, bay leaves, stock powder/bouillon and yeast extract and bring to the boil. Turn down the heat to the lowest setting and simmer for 40 minutes with the lid on. Stir about halfway through to ensure the onions are not sticking and add more water if necessary.

To make the cashew cheese, drain the soaked cashews and add to a blender with the almond milk, tapioca flour, nutritional yeast, garlic powder and salt. Blitz together to make a smooth paste, then pour into a small pan. Heat gently and stir well until the mixture thickens and becomes nice and gooey. Add more water as needed – if it cools and sets, just reheat and whisk back into a gooey mixture.

Check the seasoning in both the soup and the cashew cheese, and add more salt where needed.

Ladle the soup into deep bowls, top each with a thick slice of toasted baguette and drizzle with a spoonful or two of the cashew cheese. Add a sprinkle of freshly snipped chives, if you like, before serving.

ROASTED TOMATO SOUP
WITH PAPRIKA TORTILLA STRAWS

Tomato soup is a British comfort food classic. For me, and now my own children, it represents childhood comfort food. It's what mum used to make me when I needed looking after. Of course, there are other variations, but for many people, only the one that comes out of the famous red can will ever be good enough.

FOR THE SOUP

2 kg/4½ lbs. fresh ripe tomatoes
3 small red onions, quartered
6 whole garlic cloves, skins on
1 tablespoon vegetable oil
1.5 litres/quarts vegetable stock
1–2 teaspoons salt, to taste
1 teaspoon freshly ground white
    pepper

FOR THE PAPRIKA STRAWS

2 flour tortillas
1 tablespoon freshly chopped thyme
1 tablespoon mild paprika
1 teaspoon salt
pinch of chilli/chili powder (optional)
60 ml/¼ cup pomace oil

FOR THE BASIL OIL

handful of basil leaves
200 ml/scant 1 cup extra virgin
    olive oil
½ teaspoon salt

TO SERVE

vegan cream (optional)

2 large baking sheets, very lightly oiled

SERVES 3–4

Preheat the oven to 200°C (400°F) Gas 6.

Using a small, sharp paring knife, remove the top part of the hard core from each of the tomatoes. Place the tomatoes on one of the prepared baking sheets, tops facing up. On the second baking sheet, lay the onion quarters and garlic cloves and drizzle with the oil. Place both baking sheets in the oven and roast for 40 minutes. Remove the onions and garlic cloves, but continue to cook the tomatoes for a further 20 minutes until completely softened and sticky. Set aside to cool.

Reduce the oven to 140°C (275°F) Gas 1 for the paprika straws.

To make the paprika straws, using a large, sharp knife, slice the tortillas into quarters, then slice them into strips, 3–4 mm/⅛ inch wide. In a large bowl, mix the thyme, paprika, salt and chilli/chili powder, if using. Add the tortilla strips and toss until well covered. Drizzle with the oil and toss again until well coated.

Lay the tortilla strips on a baking sheet in a single layer and bake in the low oven for 20 minutes until golden brown and crispy. Remove from the oven and transfer to paper towels to cool and drain off any excess oil.

Meanwhile, using your hands, squeeze out the garlic from their skins and discard the skins. Then remove and discard the skins from the tomatoes (you can leave the skins on if you prefer or want to save time). Tip the onions, garlic and tomatoes into a large, deep pan and add the stock. Using a stick blender, purée the soup until smooth. Bring to the boil, then simmer on low heat for 10 minutes. Add the salt and pepper to taste.

To make the basil oil, combine the fresh basil with the extra virgin olive oil and salt in a food processor or blender, then blitz until completely smooth. This will keep for several weeks in a clean bottle in the fridge.

Serve the warm soup in big bowls, with a pile of crispy paprika tortilla straws on top and drizzled with basil oil and vegan cream, if using.

DEEP DIJON PIE
WITH OLIVE OIL MASH

Like most Northerners, I love pie. But as much as I love a good cheese and onion pie, I wanted to make one that doesn't rely on dairy. Mustard is a global crowd-pleaser and Dijon is one of my favourites, making this creamy filling feel indulgent. I think pies should be indulgent. That's why I wanted it to have a good pastry-to-filling ratio, so a deep pie dish is absolutely essential. The pastry for this satisfying deep-filled pie is based on Michel Roux's pâte brisée. I have experimented with numerous vegan substitutions for his pastry recipes, and I find that silken tofu makes a great egg replacement. Silken tofu has a fantastic texture for making dough or even vegan quiche.

FOR THE PASTRY
150 g/5½ oz. vegan 'margarine' such
    as Stork (or coconut butter)
250 g/scant 2 cups plain/all-purpose
    flour, plus extra for dusting
pinch of caster/superfine sugar
1 teaspoon salt
1 tablespoon almond milk, plus extra
    for brushing
50 g/1¾ oz. silken tofu

MAKES 450 G/1 LB.

FOR THE PIE
1 quantity vegan pastry (see above)
1 medium potato, peeled and diced
1 large carrot, peeled and diced
¼ cauliflower, cut into 1 cm/
    ½-inch florets
3 tablespoons vegetable oil
1 heaped tablespoon plain/
    all-purpose flour

350 ml/1½ cups almond milk
2 heaped tablespoons Dijon mustard
50 ml/3½ tablespoons almond cream
2 banana shallots, finely chopped
2 garlic cloves, minced
1 celery stick, diced
1 leek, sliced into 5-mm/¼-inch slices
    and washed
sea salt and freshly ground white
    pepper, to taste

FOR THE MASH
6–7 large Maris Piper or Yukon Gold
    potatoes, peeled and quartered
4–6 tablespoons good-quality virgin
    olive oil (I use Sicilian)
1–2 teaspoons rock or sea salt, to taste
1 teaspoon freshly ground white pepper

TO SERVE
steamed greens and broccoli

1 deep pie dish or 4 individual pie dishes,
    oiled
baking beans

SERVES 4

To prepare the pastry, rub the margarine, flour, sugar and salt together to make a rough crumb, then add the milk and tofu to form a soft dough. Knead gently, then wrap in clingfilm/plastic wrap and place in the fridge for 20 minutes.

Preheat the oven to 160°C (325°F) Gas 3.

If using four small pie dishes, divide the dough into four portions. Flour a surface and roll out the pastry to 3–4 mm/⅛ inch thick. Lay gently over the pie dish and gently but firmly push the pastry into the sides, ensuring there are no gaps and the pastry hangs over the top of the dish. Trim the excess pastry but leave a 2-cm/¾-inch overhang to allow for shrinkage. Keep the trimmed pastry for making the pie top(s) later. Place in the fridge for 10–15 minutes.

Cover the pastry with a sheet of baking parchment and fill with baking beans. Bake for 20 minutes (aim to cook the pastry without colouring). Remove the baking parchment and beans and return the pastry to the oven for 5 minutes. Remove from the oven and set aside. Increase the oven temperature to 180°C (350°F) Gas 4.

To make the filling, parboil diced the potato for 10 minutes until just soft. Parboil the carrot and cauliflower for 3–4 minutes until just soft. Drain and set aside.

Add 2 tablespoons of the vegetable oil to a deep frying pan/skillet and put over a medium heat. Add the flour and mix together to form a roux. Slowly add the almond milk, whisking constantly to make a thick, smooth white sauce. Add the Dijon mustard and almond cream and season to taste. Set aside.

Add the chopped shallots to a large pan, along with the remaining 1 tablespoon of vegetable oil. Fry for 5 minutes until just softened and translucent, then add the garlic, celery and leek and cook for another 3–4 minutes, until all the vegetables are well cooked and soft. Remove from the heat. Combine the shallot mixture with the parboiled vegetables and the creamy Dijon sauce. Mix well.

Fill the pastry case(s) with the vegetable mixture. Roll out the remaining pastry on a floured surface and cut out one large or four small rounds to fit the top of your pie dish(es). Brush with almond milk and use a fork to crimp the edges. Put the pie(s) on a baking sheet and bake for 20–25 minutes until golden.

Meanwhile, to make the mash, boil the potatoes until soft. Drain in a colander for 5 minutes. Mash them until smooth. Add the olive oil, salt and pepper, and, using a whisk, whip until creamy. Taste to check the seasoning; add more salt if needed. Serve the pies with the mash and steamed greens and broccoli.

ROASTED AUBERGINE LASAGNE
WITH PUY LENTILS

We love a good vegetarian lasagne in our house. I don't think you can beat a homemade one. I think the dish benefits from being left overnight and baked the following day, but a few hours in the fridge will do the job if pushed for time. The lentils can be substituted for vegan 'mince' and the aubergines/eggplants for courgettes/zucchini, if you like.

FOR THE LENTIL MIXTURE

2 tablespoons olive oil
1 large onion, diced
4 garlic cloves, crushed
250 g/generous 1¼ cups Puy lentils
750 ml/3¼ cups vegetable stock, plus extra if needed
12 large tomatoes
1 carrot, diced
1 red (bell) pepper deseeded and diced
1 celery stick, diced
2 tablespoons dark soy sauce
1 bay leaf
handful of fresh marjoram
handful of fresh thyme
2 tablespoons tomato purée/paste
½ teaspoon salt, or to taste
½ teaspoon freshly ground black pepper, or to taste

FOR THE AUBERGINE/ EGGPLANT LAYER

2 aubergines/eggplants
2 tablespoons olive oil

FOR THE 'BÉCHAMEL'

2 tablespoons olive oil
½ teaspoon salt, or to taste
½ teaspoon ground white pepper, or to taste
2 tablespoons plain/ all-purpose flour
400 ml/scant 1¾ cups almond or soy milk
1 bay leaf
½ teaspoon mustard powder

TO ASSEMBLE

1 packet of egg-free lasagne sheets
120 g/4½ oz. grated vegan Italian-style hard cheese

SERVES 6–8

Start with the lentil mixture. Heat 1 tablespoon of the olive oil in a pan and sauté half of the onion and one crushed garlic clove until softened. Add the Puy lentils and sauté for a further minute, then add the stock and simmer until the lentils are fully cooked and soft. Add further stock as needed; you are aiming for the lentils to absorb most of the liquid without leaving too much broth.

Preheat the oven to 200°C (400°F) Gas 6.

Remove the hard cores from the tomatoes. Place them whole on a baking sheet, along with the 3 remaining crushed garlic cloves and roast in the oven until well roasted and almost starting to blacken. Blitz with a stick blender and set aside.

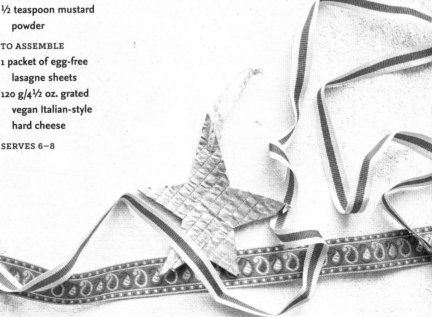

To make the aubergine/eggplant layer, remove the ends of the aubergines/eggplants. Slice them lengthways into 1 cm/½ inch thick slices. Place on a baking sheet, drizzle with the olive oil and season. Roast in the oven until golden brown and soft. Set aside.

Reduce the oven temperature to 190°C (375°F) Gas 5.

Back to the lentil mixture. Heat the remaining 1 tablespoon of olive oil in a pan and sauté the remaining half of the onion, along with the carrot, red (bell) pepper and celery, then add the cooked lentil mixture, soy sauce, bay leaf, and fresh marjoram and thyme. Add the blended tomatoes and the tomato purée/paste. Bring to the boil and simmer for 10 minutes. Add the salt and pepper, then adjust the seasoning according to taste.

To make the 'béchamel', heat the olive oil in a small, deep pan, add the salt, white pepper and flour, and cook to make a roux. Gently cook the paste for 2–3 minutes. Slowly add the milk, whisking all the time, until it reaches a creamy sauce consistency. Add the bay leaf and the mustard powder, and simmer for 2–3 minutes. Check the seasoning.

Layer some 'béchamel' sauce in the bottom of a large, deep baking dish and cover with lasagne sheets. Add half of the lentil and tomato mixture, followed by a layer of aubergine/eggplant, using all the slices and overlapping them to create a thick layer. Add the remaining lentil mixture, a final layer of lasagne sheets and top with the remaining 'béchamel'. Sprinkle with the vegan cheese and some salt and pepper.

Bake for 30–40 minutes until bubbling and the top is golden brown. Serve.

FAUX FISH PIE
WITH HERBY MASH

This hearty comfort dish brings together those familiar seafood pie flavours with some great vegan alternatives. I wanted to recreate the distinctive flaky, smoky and sweet flavours and have ramped up the flavours in the mash and the velvety sauce. Substitute or leave out some of the faux fish alternatives if you find they are difficult to get hold of.

2–3 tablespoons olive oil

3 banana shallots, finely chopped

1 carrot, finely diced

1 small leek, thinly sliced

2 tablespoons plain/all-purpose flour

300 ml/1¼ cups vegan milk

250 ml/1 cup plus 1 tablespoon good-quality vegetable stock

2 bay leaves

1 teaspoon smoked essence

10 g/¼ oz. dried dulse seaweed, soaked in boiling water (I also use a dried seaweed mix)

1 x 410-g/14-oz. can heart of palm, drained and rinsed (or use artichoke hearts), roughly chopped

4 vegan 'prawns/shrimp', roughly sliced at an angle

2 vegan 'scallop' balls, roughly chopped into 1–2 cm/½–¾ inch pieces

100 g/3½ oz. fresh chard leaves, roughly chopped (or use spinach leaves)

large handful of freshly chopped dill

½–1 teaspoon sea salt

FOR THE HERBY MASH

6 large white potatoes, such as Maris Piper, peeled and quartered

4 tablespoons good-quality olive oil

60 ml/¼ cup vegan crème fraîche or cream

1–2 teaspoons fine sea salt, to taste

1 teaspoon freshly ground white pepper

½ large bunch of parsley, freshly chopped

80 g/scant 1 cup grated vegan hard cheese (optional)

large handful of fresh breadcrumbs (optional)

small handful of pumpkin seeds (optional)

lemon wedges, to serve

SERVES 5–6

First, make the herby mash. Half-fill a large pan with water, cover and bring to the boil. Add the potatoes and boil for 20–30 minutes until completely soft. Drain into a colander and leave to drain and cool for 5–10 minutes. Put the potatoes back into the empty pan and add the olive oil. Mash vigorously, adding the crème fraîche or cream, salt and pepper, and whipping a little to make it smooth and creamy. Add the parsley and mix well. Set aside.

Preheat the oven to 180°C (350°F) Gas 4.

Put the olive oil into a deep frying pan/skillet, add the shallots and fry very gently, taking care not to colour them, for 8–10 minutes until translucent and sticky. Add the carrot and leek, and fry for a further 6–7 minutes. Add the flour to the pan and mix well to make a chunky roux. Add the milk, mix well and continue to heat gently for a few minutes, stirring. Add the stock, bay leaves, smoked essence and seaweed to the pan, stirring well. Add all the remaining ingredients, season with the salt to taste, stir well and cook gently until the greens are wilted. Pour the mixture into a deep baking dish. Top with the herby mash, then sprinkle with the grated cheese, breadcrumbs and pumpkin seeds, if using.

Put the pie in the centre of the preheated oven, with a baking sheet underneath to catch any sauce bubbling over. Bake for 30–40 minutes until golden and crispy on top and the sides are bubbling.

Allow to stand for 5 minutes before serving with lemon wedges, if you like.

SAFFRON RAVIOLI
WITH HEART OF PALM & CHILLI

The pasta dough in this recipe uses aquafaba, or chickpea water, as an alternative to eggs. This makes a great Italian-inspired dinner, and will surprise your seafood-loving friends.

FOR THE PASTA DOUGH

250 ml/1 cup plus 1 tablespoon aquafaba 'egg' (see page 138)
generous pinch of saffron threads
300 g/2¼ cups 'oo' flour, plus extra for dusting

FOR THE FILLING

½ x 410-g/14½-oz. can heart of palm, drained and chopped or use palm centres only using 1 can
1 tablespoon freshly chopped parsley
1 small garlic clove, finely chopped
2 tablespoons vegan cream cheese
½ teaspoon sea salt

TO SERVE

2–3 tablespoons good-quality olive oil
2 small garlic cloves, crushed but with skin left on
1–2 teaspoons dried chilli flakes/ hot red pepper flakes
½–1 teaspoon fine sea salt, to taste

MAKES APPROX. 12–15 LARGE RAVIOLI

To make the pasta dough, pour the aquafaba into a small pan, put over a high heat and bring to the boil. Add the saffron and simmer for 8–10 minutes until the liquid is reduced by at least a third. Set aside to cool. In a large bowl, add the flour and about 100 ml/⅓ cup plus 1 tablespoon of the aquafaba. Add up to another 50 ml/3½ tablespoons of the aquafaba. Using your hands, bring the dough together to make a firm but pliable dough. Knead for 5–10 minutes, and then cover with a damp kitchen towel and leave to rest for an hour or so at room temperature.

For the filling, in a small bowl, add the heart of palm. Squeeze out any excess water and then mix in the parsley, garlic and the vegan cream cheese. Mix well and season with the salt. Set aside.

Divide the dough into three pieces. Roll out one piece to about 3 mm/⅛ inch thick and 40.5 x 25 cm/16 x 10 inches in size and slice in half lengthways, to make two large strips, each 12.5 cm/5 inches wide.

Lay the pasta sheets on a lightly floured surface. Place 4–5 tablespoonfuls of the filling mixture in a line along one of the sheets. Brush the pasta around the filling with a little of the remaining aquafaba, then lay another pasta sheet over the top and, using your hand, gently push out any air before sealing. Use a cookie cutter to cut out 4–5 circular pieces. Cover the pieces with a kitchen towel while you finish the remaining ravioli making 12–15 large pieces, in total.

To cook the ravioli, put a large, deep pan over a high heat and half-fill with water. Bring to a rolling boil and then gently place the ravioli into the water. Bring back to the boil and reduce to a simmer, cooking for 5 minutes until the ravioli floats. Carefully lift the cooked ravioli out using a slotted spoon, and lay in a wide sieve/strainer on paper towels to drain.

In a small frying pan/skillet, add the olive oil and crushed garlic cloves. Fry over a medium-high heat for a minute or two, then add the dried chilli flakes/hot red pepper flakes and salt to taste. Sauté for a further 2–3 minutes, then remove from the heat and discard the garlic. Put the ravioli pieces on a serving plate, drizzle over the chilli/chile oil and serve immediately.

CHEESY CHKN, LEEK & MUSHROOM PIE

This big flaky-topped pie will serve a hungry party of six. I love this pie for many reasons. It's easy to find vegan chicken substitutes at the local shops (or use the recipe for homemade seitan chicken on page 140). And the recipe takes less than 30 minutes to prepare. The unbaked pie also freezes really well for several months, so I often make two at the same time, or several smaller ones to freeze for another time. I don't think anything beats homemade ready-made food!

FOR THE SAUCE

120 g/1 cup cashews, soaked in cold water for 3 hours

500 ml/generous 2 cups almond or soya/soy milk

9 g/1 heaped tablespoon tapioca starch

4 tablespoons nutritional yeast

1 teaspoon garlic powder

½–1 teaspoon sea salt, to taste

FOR THE FILLING

2 tablespoons olive oil

2 shallots, finely chopped

2–3 leeks, thickly sliced

200 g/7 oz. chkn pieces (see page 140) or use ready-made vegan pieces

225 g/8 oz. chestnut mushrooms, cleaned and halved

½ bunch of freshly snipped chives

1 tablespoon Dijon mustard

1 x 500-g/18-oz. packet ready-made vegan puff pastry

plain/all-purpose flour, for dusting

2–3 tablespoons vegan milk, for glazing

SERVES 4–6

Preheat the oven to 190°C (375°F) Gas 5.

Drain and rinse the soaked cashew nuts, and add to a blender with all the other ingredients for the sauce. Blitz together to make a smooth paste, then pour into a small saucepan. Heat gently over a low heat and stir well until the mixture thickens.

For the filling, add the olive oil to a large, deep pan and put over a medium heat. Add the shallots and leeks and cook for 10–12 minutes until soft and translucent. Add the vegan chkn pieces, mushrooms, chives, mustard and cashew sauce. Stir well, then pour into a large baking dish, or several small ones.

Roll out the pastry on a well-floured surface, and put on top of the pie filling. Trim and pinch the edges. Using a pastry brush, dip into the vegan milk and brush the top(s) of the pastry before baking. Make 2–3 small holes to allow the steam to escape.

Place on the middle shelf of the preheated oven and bake for 40–50 minutes until the pastry is crispy and golden brown. Serve immediately.

CAULIFLOWER MAC 'N' JACK
WITH CRISPY CAPER BITES

The British staple of cauliflower cheese is often considered the ultimate way to serve cauliflower. But what do you do if you can't decide whether to have cauliflower cheese or macaroni cheese? My friend Jo said they just have both together, problem solved.

1 cauliflower, cut into large florets

200 g/7 oz. macaroni or penne pasta

1 litre/quart almond milk

2 bay leaves

few sprigs of fresh thyme

3 tablespoons pomace or vegetable oil

2 heaped tablespoons plain/
    all-purpose flour

4–5 heaped tablespoons nutritional
    yeast

3 teaspoons English/hot mustard
    (or 2 teaspoons mustard powder)

2 teaspoons onion powder

1 teaspoon sweet smoked paprika

1–2 teaspoons rock salt

½ teaspoon freshly ground white
    pepper

100 g/generous ¾ cup cashews,
    soaked in cold water for 2 hours,
    drained and blended to a fine paste

60–120 ml/¼–½ cup Jack Daniels
    (or other whiskey, optional)

1 tablespoon grated vegan Italian-
    style hard cheese (optional)

FOR THE CRISPY CAPER BITES

1–2 tablespoons capers or pitted
    green olives, roughly chopped

1 tablespoon cornflour/cornstarch

1–2 teaspoons rock salt

½ tablespoon vegetable oil

large baking sheet, lightly oiled

SERVES 4–5

Preheat the oven to 220°C (425°F) Gas 7.

Place the cauliflower florets on the oiled baking sheet and bake in the hot oven for 20 minutes until starting to turn golden and brown.

Cook the pasta according to the packet instructions, but minus 4 minutes, as the pasta will finish cooking when it is baked at the end. This way, it won't be overcooked and mushy. Keep some of the cooking water for later.

In a small pan, heat the milk gently with the bay leaves and sprigs of thyme. Bring to a gentle simmer, then remove from the heat and leave the herbs to poach.

In a deep frying pan/skillet, heat the pomace oil over a medium heat. Add the flour and whisk to make a roux, cooking gently for 2–3 minutes. Strain the infused milk into a jug/pitcher, then pour slowly into the roux, a little at a time, whisking constantly over a low heat until all the milk is combined and you have a thick and creamy sauce. Keep over low heat and add the nutritional yeast, mustard, onion powder, paprika, salt and pepper. Add the blended cashews and Jack Daniels (if using), then stir well. Remove from the heat.

Mix the cooked pasta and the sauce together, then carefully add the baked cauliflower florets and mix well. There should be plenty of sauce, so add some of the pasta liquid if needed. Tip into a large baking dish and return to the oven for 10–15 minutes.

To make the crispy caper bites, drain the capers or olives, then lay on paper towels to dry slightly. Mix together the cornflour/cornstarch and salt, and toss the capers in the seasoned flour. In a small pan, heat the vegetable oil over a medium-high heat. Check the oil is hot enough by dropping in one piece – it should sizzle immediately without burning. Gently add the capers to the pan and fry until crisp and golden. Drain on paper towels. Remove the baking dish from the oven and sprinkle the crispy caper bites over the top of the cauliflower pasta. Season with salt and black pepper and add a sprinkling of vegan cheese, if using.

ROOT VEG ROSTI

This is a great recipe for serving up less popular root vegetables, and using a muffin pan creates moreish little cakes with a lovely crispy exterior and soft pillowy insides. Serve as a side dish for a big roast dinner, and you can serve any leftovers for brunch topped with baked beans.

2 large potatoes, peeled and grated

1 parsnip, peeled and grated

½ small squash or 200 g/7 oz. pumpkin, peeled and grated

2 carrots, peeled, deseeded and grated

2 litres/quarts boiling water

2 tablespoons vegetable oil

1 large onion, finely sliced

½ tablespoon plain/all-purpose flour

½ tablespoon freshly chopped thyme (or ¼ teaspoon dried)

1–2 teaspoons salt, to taste

vegetable oil, for greasing

12-hole muffin pan

24 small squares of greaseproof paper, approximately 9 x 9 cm/ 3½ x 3½ inches

MAKES 24

Preheat the oven to 170°C (325°F) Gas 3.

Put the grated potatoes, parsnip, squash or pumpkin and carrots into a large bowl. Pour over the boiling water and leave to stand for 10 minutes.

Heat 1 tablespoon of the oil in a frying pan/skillet and sauté the onion until it turns sticky. Add the flour and cook for a further 2–3 minutes. Tip the softened onion mixture into a large, clean bowl.

Drain the grated vegetables, then, using your hands, squeeze out the excess water. (For the perfect rosti, and if you have time, you can refrigerate the grated part-cooked vegetables at this stage for a couple of hours.) Next, add the vegetables to the bowl of softened onion mixture. Add the thyme and salt to taste. Mix well.

Grease the muffin pan and line each hole with two lightly oiled squares of greaseproof paper, to make a little flower shaped cases. Take a large handful of the veg mixture, shaping into a large ball then place into the papered pan hole, pressing down gently. Repeat to fill the pan.

Place the muffin pan in the preheated oven and bake for 30 minutes, then increase the oven temperature to 180°C (350°F) Gas 4 and bake for a further 15–20 minutes until golden brown. Rosti cakes can be served immediately, kept warm or reheated later in a low oven.

MACADAMIA CRUMBLE POTS
WITH SQUASH & CHICKPEAS

I try to include something seasonal and a bit luxurious in our Christmas dinner, and I think macadamia nuts are a special treat. I particularly like any dish that can be prepared in advance, so these macadamia crumble pots are perfect for a stress-free festive dinner.

FOR THE CRUMBLE
TOPPING

120 g/scant 1 cup plain/
all-purpose flour

80 g/scant 1 cup jumbo
oats

1 teaspoon freshly
chopped thyme

½ teaspoon salt

½ teaspoon freshly
ground white pepper

80 g/3 oz. vegan
'margarine', such as
Stork, chopped into
pieces

60 g/½ cup macadamia
nuts, roughly chopped

FOR THE FILLING

1 squash, peeled,
deseeded and chopped
into 2-cm/¾-inch
cubes

1 tablespoon vegetable oil

1 small white onion,
chopped

400-g/14-oz. can
chickpeas, drained
and rinsed

1 litre/quart vegetable
stock

2 teaspoons Dijon
mustard

250 g/9 oz. fresh spinach
(or 100 g/3½ oz.
frozen)

1 tablespoon freshly
chopped thyme

4 fresh sage leaves,
finely chopped

1 teaspoon cornflour/
cornstarch

½–1 teaspoon salt,
to taste

½ teaspoon freshly
ground white pepper

1 baking sheet, lightly oiled
5–6 individual ovenproof
pots

SERVES 5–6

Preheat the oven to 200°C (400°F) Gas 6.

For the filling, put the squash onto the oiled baking sheet, drizzle over the oil, ensuring the pieces are well coated. Bake in the preheated oven for 20–30 minutes, until it is golden brown with caramelized edges. Remove from the oven and reduce the temperature to 180°C (350°F) Gas 4, if you are planning to cook the pots immediately.

Meanwhile, prepare the crumble topping by placing the flour in a large bowl. Add the oats, thyme, salt and pepper, and mix well. Add the margarine and, using your fingertips, rub the fat into the dry mixture to create a crumbly texture. Add the macadamia nuts to the crumble, mix well, then set aside.

In a large, deep frying pan/skillet or wok, sauté the onion (for the filling) for about 10–15 minutes over a low heat until soft and translucent. Add the chickpeas, stock, mustard, spinach and herbs. Bring to a simmer for a few minutes.

Mix the cornflour/cornstarch in a little water and add to the pan, so that the mixture thickens slightly, then add the roasted squash, salt and pepper. Mix well and then taste to check the level of seasoning.

Fill the pots three-quarters full with the squash filling. Then top each pot with a few tablespoons of the crumble mixture. If preparing in advance, the pots can be chilled or frozen at this stage.

To finish, place the pots on a baking sheet and bake in the preheated oven for 30–40 minutes until the crumble top is golden brown and the filling is starting to bubble underneath.

BAKED BEETROOT
& HORSERADISH MORNAY

This is a lovely accompaniment for a celebratory roast dinner. I love beetroots/beets. So did Tom Robbins it seems. He wrote a series of weird and wonderful books in the '80s and '90s (remember *Even Cowgirls Get the Blues* and Uma Thurman with her giant thumbs for hitchhiking?). One of my favourite of Robbins' books had an entire chapter dedicated to the wonders of beetroots/beets: 'The beet is the most intense of vegetables. The radish, admittedly, is more feverish, but the fire of the radish is a cold fire, the fire of discontent not of passion. Tomatoes are lusty enough, yet there runs through tomatoes an undercurrent of frivolity. Beets are deadly serious.' *Jitterbug Perfume* (1984). According to Tom, it could be the secret to immortality. I'm not sure about that, but I have noticed its resurgence on dining menus.

6 yellow and red beetroots/beets

700 ml/3 cups almond milk

2 bay leaves

7.5–10-cm/3–4-inch root of fresh horseradish, peeled and grated (or 2 tablespoons horseradish sauce from a jar)

3 tablespoons pomace oil

2 heaped tablespoons plain/ all-purpose flour

2 tablespoons nutritional yeast

1–2 teaspoons rock salt, to taste

½ teaspoon freshly ground white pepper

2 tablespoons Cashew Cream (see page 138)

1 slice brown or rye bread, blitzed to rough breadcrumbs

1 tablespoon pumpkin seeds

½ tablespoon sunflower seeds

1 tablespoon grated vegan Italian-style hard cheese

SERVES 4–5

Top and tail the beetroots/beets (do not peel) and place in a large pan of boiling water. Simmer for 30–40 minutes until fully cooked. Remove from the pan and set aside to cool.

Preheat the oven to 190°C (375°F) Gas 5.

In a small pan, heat the milk gently and add the bay leaves and grated horseradish. Bring to a gentle simmer, then remove from the heat and leave to poach.

In a deep frying pan/skillet, heat the pomace oil over a medium heat. Add the flour and whisk to make a roux, cooking gently for 2–3 minutes. Strain the milk into a jug/pitcher, then pour slowly into the roux, a little at a time, whisking constantly until all the milk is combined and you have a thick and creamy sauce. Keep over a low heat and add the nutritional yeast, salt and pepper. Add the cashew cream and stir well, then remove the sauce from the heat.

Using gloved hands, use your fingers to rub the peel from the cooked beetroots/beets. Then slice the beetroot/beets into 5 mm/ ¼ inch-thick discs.

Layer the beetroot/beet slices in a deep, ovenproof dish, and pour over the Mornay sauce. Sprinkle the breadcrumbs, seeds and cheese over the top, then bake in the oven for 20–25 minutes until the top is golden and bubbling. Serve immediately.

BORDELAISE SUET PUDDING

This dish was inspired by Crossroad Kitchen's porcini bordelaise, which has such eye-opening richness that it's truly hard to believe it is made with a vegan demi-glace. The secret to this dish is definitely in the Roasted Vegetable Stock (see page 141). The vegan demi-glace technique can be used on its own for making a super-rich wine gravy for other dishes. Make larger quantities of the demi-glace (a day before is helpful) and freeze in portions to use later. As a child growing up in the '70s and '80s, steamed suet puddings were comfort on a plate. This Bordelaise-style sauce works sublimely with the crumbly pastry.

FOR THE SUET PASTRY

250 g/scant 2 cups self-raising/self-rising flour

180 g/6½ oz. vegan suet

½ teaspoon salt

60 g/generous 1 cup fresh breadcrumbs, white or brown

½ teaspoon baking powder

125–150 ml/½–⅔ cup vegan milk, such as almond or soya/soy

FOR THE DEMI-GLACE

30 g/scant 4 tablespoons plain/all-purpose flour

3 tablespoons olive or coconut oil

1 litre/quart Roasted Vegetable Stock (see page 141)

2 bay leaves

1 teaspoon black peppercorns

1 teaspoon white peppercorns

4 sprigs of fresh rosemary

small handful of fresh thyme

2 tablespoons olive oil

1 teaspoon salt

FOR THE FILLING

3 shallots, finely chopped

240 ml/1 cup red wine, such as Syrah, plus 3 tablespoons extra

1 bay leaf

3–4 sprigs of fresh thyme

2 tablespoons olive or coconut oil

280 g/10 oz. chestnut mushrooms, cleaned and quartered

30 g/1 oz. dried porcini mushrooms or other dried wild mushrooms, soaked in boiling water for 15 minutes

¼ teaspoon salt

½ teaspoon freshly ground white pepper

small handful of freshly chopped parsley

1 sprig of rosemary, finely chopped

¼ teaspoon sugar

TO SERVE

olive oil mash

1-litre/quart pudding basin, oiled

SERVES 4

In a large bowl, mix together the pastry ingredients, reserving at least 2 tablespoons of milk to ensure the dough is not too wet. Combine with your hands and knead a little to make a firm but supple dough. Flatten into a large disc and rest for 30–40 minutes.

For the demi-glace, add the flour to a heavy-based pan and toast gently over a medium heat for 1–2 minutes. Add the oil and cook for 10–15 minutes until the roux is lightly coloured and smells nutty. Slowly add the stock, stirring constantly to make a smooth sauce. Add the remaining ingredients, reduce the heat to low and simmer for an hour until the sauce is reduced and coats the back of a spoon.

In a small pan, combine the shallots, wine, bay leaf and thyme for the filling. Bring to a simmer and cook for 10 minutes until reduced by half. Strain the wine mixture, then add 240 ml/1 cup of the strained demi-glace and mix well. The remaining demi-glace can be kept in the fridge for a few days or frozen.

In a large frying pan/skillet or wok, add the oil, chestnut mushrooms and the salt and pepper, and sauté for 6–8 minutes until the mushrooms begin to brown. Stir in the sauce to the pan, then add the remaining herbs, sugar and porcini, along with the extra 3 tablespoons of red wine. Bring to a simmer again, taste and season if needed. Set aside.

Roll out the dough to 5 mm/¼ inch thick. Line the pudding basin, trimming the edges from the top and remoulding the trimmings to make a pastry lid. Add the filling, then place the pastry lid on top. Pinch the edges to seal, then cover with parchment paper and tie with string/twine. Put the basin into a large pan with enough water to come one-third of the way up the sides. Put a lid on the pan, bring to the boil and simmer on low for 3 hours. Do not let the pan boil dry. Turn upside down onto a plate and serve.

PIGLETS IN RAFTS

These are a great alternative to Yorkshire puddings and have all the crowd-pleasing flavours of toad-in-the-hole. Because they're not actually Yorkie puds and more like a popover, these can be prepared in advance and popped into the oven to reheat just before serving. The black salt is essential for the egg-like flavour, and can be easily sourced from any Indian or Pakistani grocery store.

9 vegan mini sausages

FOR THE PUDDING BATTER

4½ tablespoons Trex vegetable fat or rapeseed/sunflower oil

150 g/1 cup plus 2 tablespoons plain/all-purpose flour

320 ml/11 fl. oz. soya/soy milk

4 tablespoons egg replacement mixture such as Orgran (1 teaspoon powder makes 2 tablespoons mixture)

2 teaspoons baking powder

¼ teaspoon bicarbonate of/ baking soda

½ teaspoon black salt

9-hole muffin pan

MAKES 9

Preheat the oven to 220°C (425°F) Gas 7.

Put ½ tablespoon of Trex or vegetable oil into each of the nine holes in the muffin pan and put into the preheated oven for 10–15 minutes, until it's piping hot.

To prepare the batter, sift the flour into a large bowl and whisk together with all the remaining batter ingredients until smooth. Whisk well to make the mixture slightly frothy. Remove the hot muffin pan from the oven and place on top of the stove.

Pour the batter mixture into the muffin pan holes, half-filling each, then top each with a mini sausage. The batter should sizzle and bubble. Carefully and quickly place the pan back in the hot oven. Bake, undisturbed, for 20–25 minutes until the batter is cooked through and crispy.

Serve as a side dish as part of a festive vegan banquet.

SEASONAL STUFFING WREATH

This is a fabulous centre piece dish, perfect for slicing at the table (and my personal favourite for leftovers sandwiches on Boxing Day). This very easy recipe can be prepared in advance, and will keep well in the fridge for three or four days. It also freezes well.

8 tablespoons good-quality olive oil

2 celery sticks, diced into 5 mm/
¼-inch pieces

2 brown onions, diced

350 g/12 oz. dried vegan sausage mix
(such as SosMix or Granovita)

2 medium or 1 large apple,
preferably Bramley or Granny
Smith, peeled, cored and diced
into 2-cm/¾-inch pieces

2 tablespoons freshly squeezed
lemon juice

4 slices seeded brown bread

4 heaped tablespoons freshly
chopped parsley

½ large orange, cut into 5 mm/
¼ inch-thick semi-circle slices

large handful of fresh sage leaves

1 teaspoon salt

large handful of fresh cranberries

8 or 9 small sprigs of rosemary

Savarin mould or flan or tart pan
approximately 25–30 cm/
10–12 inches diameter, greased
with vegan margarine or oil

SERVES 6–8

Preheat the oven to 180°C (350°F) Gas 4.

Put a large frying pan/skillet on a medium heat and add a tablespoon or two of the olive oil. Add the celery and onions and sauté for 20–30 minutes until soft and translucent, stirring occasionally.

Meanwhile, put the dried sausage mixture in a large bowl and add boiling water according to packet instructions. Add 2 tablespoons of olive oil and mix well. Set aside for 10–15 minutes.

Put the apples into a bowl with the lemon juice and toss to mix.

Blitz the bread slices in a food processor to make fine breadcrumbs. Put in a large bowl with the parsley, apple pieces (and lemon juice) and the sausage mixture. Using your hands, combine well.

Lay the orange slices around the sides of the greased savarin mould, then fill with the stuffing mixture. Alternatively, if using a flan or tart pan, lay the mixture in the pan in a large, thick circle to make a wreath shape. Use your hands to shape the mixture, making a large doughnut shape with a large hole in the middle. The wreath should be approx. 7.5–10 cm/ 3–4 inches in height (if shaping by hand). If preparing in advance, this is the stage at which to cover and refrigerate or freeze the dish.

If not using a savarin mould, place the remaining orange halves face-down in the middle of the sausage wreath to stop the hole closing up. Place the other slices around the outside edge.

Cover with foil (whether using a mould or shaping by hand) and put the wreath in the preheated oven for 50–55 minutes. Remove the foil and return to the oven for a further 10–15 minutes until firm to touch.

Meanwhile, pour the remaining olive oil into a small frying pan/ skillet and put over a high heat. Add the sage leaves and salt, and fry quickly for a few minutes.

Remove the wreath from the oven. If using a savarin mould, carefully turn out onto a serving platter. Pour over the sage and olive oil, covering the sausage mixture well. Garnish the top with the cranberries, securing in place with cocktail sticks/toothpicks if needed. Garnish the centre with the sprigs of rosemary. Cover with foil to keep warm before serving.

CHARGRILLED HISPI CABBAGE
WITH VEGAN XO SAUCE

XO sauce is one of the ultimate Asian condiments created in Hong Kong and made from a mixture of umami rich seafood. This vegan version is much quicker to prepare than the traditional seafood version and can be slathered or dolloped atop a variety of vegetables.

1 hispi or sweetheart cabbage

1 small red cabbage

FOR THE XO SAUCE

50 g/1¾ oz. dried shiitake mushrooms (rehydrated with boiling water)

30 g/1 oz. dried porcini mushrooms (rehydrated in boiling water)

4 tablespoons sesame oil (not toasted)

3 shallots, finely chopped

2–3 tablespoons sunflower, rapeseed or other vegetable oil

4 plump garlic cloves, crushed

1½ tablespoons minced fresh ginger

1 sheet of nori seaweed

1 scant tablespoon fermented black beans, finely chopped

4 dried chillies/chiles, roughly chopped

2 tablespoons rice vinegar

2 teaspoons white sugar or 1½ tablespoons agave syrup

100 ml/generous ⅓ cup soy sauce

120 ml/½ cup Shaoxing wine or substitute dry sherry

½ teaspoon freshly ground black pepper

½ cinnamon stick or pinch of ground cinnamon

seeds from 1 star anise, lightly crushed

1 lemon or lime, cut into small wedges, to garnish (optional)

MAKES APPROX. 400 ML/14 FL. OZ. JAR OF SAUCE

SERVES 8–10

Preheat the oven to 200°C (400°F) Gas 6.

Carefully remove the mushrooms from the soaking water, so that any grit is left behind at the bottom. Roughly chop the rehydrated mushrooms and place in a large bowl along with 1 tablespoon of the sesame oil. Mix together so the mushrooms are well coated in the oil. Lay onto a non-stick baking sheet and bake in the preheated oven for 15–20 minutes until lightly roasted. Set aside.

Meanwhile, in a large frying pan/skillet, add the shallots with 2 tablespoons of the vegetable oil. Place on a low heat and sauté, without browning, for 20–30 minutes, until translucent and softened. Add the garlic and ginger and cook for a further 5 minutes.

Chop the nori seaweed. Add the remaining ingredients to the pan including the remaining sesame oil and seaweed (but not the lemon or lime wedges) and cook gently for 8–10 minutes. Add the roasted mushrooms and mix well. Remove from the heat and place the mixture into a blender, removing cinnamon stick if using (or use a stick blender). Carefully pulse the blender to mash the mixture a little more, but keep it slightly chunky by pulsing for a few seconds at a time. Add a tablespoon or two of soy sauce so the mixture is not too dry. Store the sauce in a sterilized jar. The sauce can be kept in the fridge for several weeks.

Remove the loose outer leaves of the cabbages, and cut the cabbages into four or eight wedges, depending on size. Do not remove the inner core as this holds the leaves together. Lightly brush the cabbage with the remaining oil.

Put a cast iron ridged griddle pan over a high heat, or use a baking sheet under a very hot grill/broiler. Put the cabbage wedges onto the pan and sear for 4–5 minutes until the edges are blackened and the cabbage starts to soften and cook through. Turn once and cook for another 4–5 minutes on the other side. Remove the cabbage wedges and arrange on a serving plate or platter. Place a teaspoon of XO vegan sauce on top of the wedge, and serve with pieces of lemon or lime.

SMOKY STUFFED ROAST
WITH PINE NUT, LEMON & HERB STUFFING

Home-smoking is very easy and adds a deep layer of flavour to lots of dishes, including home-made vegan meats or cheeses. I use a large lidded pan (only used for smoking) and a steamer basket – the kind that makes a raised layer and adjusts to the size of the pan. Smoking chips are available from cook shops or online. You can cheat by adding smoked essence to the mixture, but this doesn't infuse in the same flavourful way as actual smoking.

FOR THE ROASTING PAN
1 litre/quart vegetable stock
2 onions, quartered, skin on
1 glass of white wine (optional)
2 tablespoons soy sauce
handful of fresh herbs, such
   as thyme and rosemary
1 garlic bulb, halved
1–2 lemons, halved
1 tablespoon olive or vegetable oil
2 tablespoons balsamic vinegar

FOR THE STUFFING
2 tablespoons olive oil
2 small onions, diced
4 garlic cloves, crushed
2 slices white or brown bread
12 fresh sage leaves, finely chopped
½ teaspoon chopped zest and
   freshly squeezed juice of
   ½ lemon
½–1 teaspoon salt
½ teaspoon freshly ground
   black pepper
50 g/⅓ cup pine nuts

FOR THE ROAST
400 g/14 oz. vital wheat gluten flour
45 g/⅓ cup chickpea/gram flour
2 teaspoons garlic powder
2 tablespoons nutritional yeast
1 tablespoon onion powder
2 teaspoons Herbamere seasoning
1 teaspoon dried mixed herbs
60 ml/¼ cup tahini
280–400 ml/10–14 fl. oz. vegetable
   stock
2 teaspoons smoked essence
   (optional)

FOR THE DRY RUB
1 teaspoon freshly ground
   white pepper
1 teaspoon freshly ground
   black pepper
2 teaspoons dried herbs
1 teaspoon salt

large muslin/cheesecloth sheet,
   approx. 60 cm/24 inches square
string or twine
foil and large handful of smoking
   chips (or substitute 3 teaspoons
   smoked essence)
large lidded pan and metal
   steamerbasket

SERVES 7–8

Preheat the oven to 180°C (350°F) Gas 4.

Add all the roasting pan ingredients into a large, deep roasting pan with 1 litre/quart of water and set aside.

To make the stuffing, in a large frying pan/skillet, add the olive oil, onions and garlic and fry over a low heat for about 8–10 minutes until well softened. Turn up the heat to medium-high and continue to fry the mixture so that the onions start to brown slightly. Remove the pan from the heat and tip the contents into a large, heatproof bowl. Leave to cool.

Blitz the slices of bread in a food processor to make fine breadcrumbs. Add these to the stuffing mixture, along with the sage, lemon zest and juice, salt and pepper. Roughly chop the pine nuts and add to the bowl. Mix well with your hands. Set aside.

To make the roast, mix together the dry ingredients in a medium bowl. In a jug/pitcher, mix together the tahini and stock (add the smoked essence at this point if using). Make a well in the centre of the bowl, and pour in two thirds of the stock mixture. Combine the ingredients to make a stiff dough. Add the remaining liquid if needed; the dough should be nice and firm. Knead well for a minute or two, then leave to rest for 5–10 minutes.

Place the dough on the work surface and roll out to an oblong shape about 2–3 cm/¾–1¼ inches thick. It is very springy to work with so you will need to be patient and firm. Mix together the dry rub ingredients and scatter on the work surface. Place the flattened dough piece onto the dry rub. Press down slightly, then lift and place, rub-side down, onto a very well-oiled muslin/cheesecloth sheet.

Scoop up the stuffing using your hands and make a fat sausage shape of stuffing down the centre of the dough. Carefully roll the gluten dough up around the stuffing, using the muslin/cheesecloth to help you. Try to seal the ends as much as possible. Twist the ends of the cloth

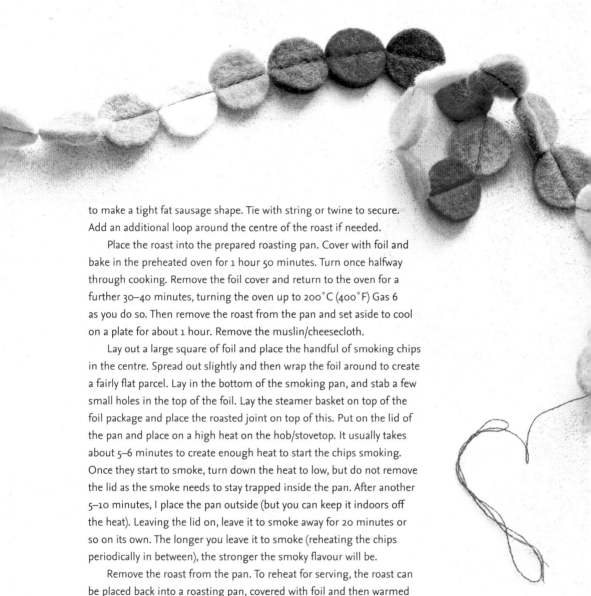

to make a tight fat sausage shape. Tie with string or twine to secure. Add an additional loop around the centre of the roast if needed.

Place the roast into the prepared roasting pan. Cover with foil and bake in the preheated oven for 1 hour 50 minutes. Turn once halfway through cooking. Remove the foil cover and return to the oven for a further 30–40 minutes, turning the oven up to 200°C (400°F) Gas 6 as you do so. Then remove the roast from the pan and set aside to cool on a plate for about 1 hour. Remove the muslin/cheesecloth.

Lay out a large square of foil and place the handful of smoking chips in the centre. Spread out slightly and then wrap the foil around to create a fairly flat parcel. Lay in the bottom of the smoking pan, and stab a few small holes in the top of the foil. Lay the steamer basket on top of the foil package and place the roasted joint on top of this. Put on the lid of the pan and place on a high heat on the hob/stovetop. It usually takes about 5–6 minutes to create enough heat to start the chips smoking. Once they start to smoke, turn down the heat to low, but do not remove the lid as the smoke needs to stay trapped inside the pan. After another 5–10 minutes, I place the pan outside (but you can keep it indoors off the heat). Leaving the lid on, leave it to smoke away for 20 minutes or so on its own. The longer you leave it to smoke (reheating the chips periodically in between), the stronger the smoky flavour will be.

Remove the roast from the pan. To reheat for serving, the roast can be placed back into a roasting pan, covered with foil and then warmed in the oven at 160°C (325°F) Gas 3 for 10–15 minutes, or warmed in the microwave on High for 2–3 minutes. Serve in thick slices with mashed potato and miso gravy.

CELEBRATION WELLINGTON

The Wellington is an instantly recognisable sign of a celebratory feast. It's an impressive dish to bring to the table too. There are a lot of steps in this recipe, so it's definitely one for the more skilled cook. The roast in the middle can be served without all the pastry fanfare, too, for a more straightforward recipe. I usually make at least two of the roasts, and freeze one for up to 2 months.

FOR THE ROAST

500 g/18 oz. vital wheat gluten flour

45 g/⅓ cup chickpea/gram flour

5 tablespoons flavourless coconut oil

2 banana shallots, finely chopped

1 medium leek, finely chopped

150 g/5½ oz. chestnut mushrooms, finely chopped

150 g/5½ oz. field or Portobello mushrooms, finely chopped

6 garlic cloves, finely chopped

2 teaspoons garlic powder

3 g/⅛ oz. dried porcini or wild mushrooms, soaked in 100 ml/ ⅓ cup plus 1 tablespoon boiling water

1 tablespoon tomato purée/paste

2 teaspoons sea salt

½ tablespoon Marmite or other yeast extract

1½ tablespoons dark soy sauce

4 bay leaves

1 teaspoon smoked essence

1 small glass of robust red wine, such as Syrah (approx. 100 ml/ ⅓ cup plus 1 tablespoon)

150 ml plus 50 ml/⅔ cup plus 3½ tablespoons Roasted Vegetable Stock (see page 141)

FOR THE ROASTING PAN

450 ml/scant 2 cups good-quality vegetable stock

2 small onions, quartered, skins left on

1 small glass of robust red wine, such as Syrah (approx. 100 ml/ ⅓ cup plus 1 tablespoon)

2 tablespoons soy sauce

handful of fresh thyme

2–3 sprigs of fresh rosemary

1 tablespoon olive or vegetable oil

1 tablespoon balsamic vinegar

FOR THE DRY RUB

2 teaspoons freshly ground black pepper

2 teaspoons paprika

1 teaspoon ground white pepper

2 teaspoons dried mixed herbs

FOR THE PÂTÉ

250 g/9 oz. field, Portobello or chestnut mushrooms, cleaned

handful of fresh parsley

80 g/⅔ cup pecans, lightly toasted (or use walnuts)

40 g/3 tablespoons vegan margarine

salt and freshly ground white pepper, to taste

FOR THE PANCAKES

125 g/1 cup minus 1 tablespoon plain/ all-purpose flour

1 flax 'egg' (see page 138)

240 ml/1 cup unsweetened soya/ soy milk

flavourless coconut oil or vegetable oil, for frying

1 x 500-g/18-oz. packet of ready-made vegan puff pastry

4 tablespoons soya/soy milk

1 teaspoon black poppy seeds

plain/all-purpose flour, for dusting

1 large muslin/cheesecloth sheet, approx. 60 cm/24 inches square, lightly oiled

string or twine for tying

SERVES 7–8

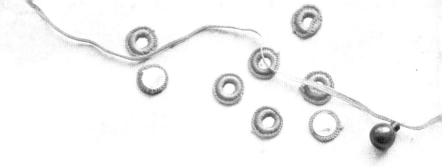

For the roast, put the gluten and chickpea/gram flour into a large mixing bowl. Mix together and set aside.

In a medium frying pan/skillet, add half of the coconut oil, the shallots and leek, then place over a medium heat. Sauté for 7–9 minutes to soften the vegetables, then add the mushrooms and fresh and powdered garlic. Chop the soaked dried mushrooms and add them along with the soaking liquid to the pan. Cook for 6–7 minutes, then add the remaining coconut oil, the tomato purée/paste, salt, Marmite/yeast extract, soy sauce, bay leaves, smoked essence and red wine. Bring to a simmer, stirring well, then reduce the liquid by half on a high heat for another 5–10 minutes, then set aside to cool.

Preheat the oven to 180°C (350°F) Gas 4. Add all the roasting pan ingredients into a large, deep roasting pan and set aside.

Add the mushroom mixture along with the 150 ml/⅔ cup vegetable stock to the gluten and chickpea/gram flour, mixing well to make a very stiff dough. Add the extra stock if needed, depending on the flour density and mushrooms. The stiffer the dough, the firmer the texture of the vegan 'meat'. Knead well for a few minutes to ensure it is well mixed. You can also use a stand mixer and dough hook for this. Roll the dough into a large, thick roast shape and then leave to rest for about 10 minutes.

Mix together the dry rub ingredients and scatter on the work surface. Roll the dough in this dry rub, then lay on the lightly oiled muslin/cheesecloth and roll so the roast is snugly wrapped in the cloth. Tie each end with string or twine. Tie further loops around the roast to ensure it is fairly tightly wrapped and secure. Lay the roast in the prepared roasting pan, cover the pan with foil and place in the oven for 2 hours. Turn once halfway through cooking. Remove the foil and return to the oven for further 30–40 minutes, then remove and set aside to cool slightly for about an hour. Then remove the muslin/cheesecloth.

Preheat the oven to 120°C (250°F) Gas ½. To make the pâté, lay
the mushrooms on a dry baking sheet and place in the oven for
30–40 minutes, occasionally draining away the liquid from the baking
sheet. Once roasted and fairly dry-looking, blitz together with the
parsley, pecans and margarine using a food processor or stick blender.
Season with salt and pepper to taste. Set aside in the fridge to chill.

Make the pancakes by whisking together the flour, flax 'egg' and
soya/soy milk. In a small frying pan/skillet, add a knob of coconut oil
or a little vegetable oil and place over a high heat. Pour a small amount
of batter into the pan, using a spatula to spread the batter thinly across
the base of the pan. Cook for a few minutes on each side. Set aside to
cool on paper towels. Repeat.

Roll out the puff pastry to a rectangle of about 3–4 mm/⅛ inch
thickness. Lay the pancakes over the top of the pastry, so they are slightly
overlapping and cover most of the pastry apart from the edges. Thickly
spread the mushroom pâté over the pancakes, then gently lay the roast
in the centre. Wrap the pancake and pastry layers around the roast,
using the soya/soy milk to seal. Trim the pastry to make neatly folded
ends. Glaze the outside of the pastry with soya/soy milk. Sprinkle with
the poppy seeds, and score the pastry if you like. Set on a baking sheet
and place in the preheated oven at 180°C (350°F) Gas 4 for 20–30 minutes
until the pastry is puffed and crisp.

Strain the roasting pan juices into a small pan and bring to a
simmer with a little flour to thicken if needed. Once the roast is cooked,
carve and serve.

JERUSALEM ARTICHOKES
WITH GARLIC CREAM & HAZELNUT CRUST

I tend to be led by flavours in food first rather than their health-giving properties, but it's always a small joy to find out something I love is also very good for me. And I do love hazelnuts. This dish is rich and unctuous, and feels like a treat especially when served with crusty bread and steamed broccoli. The creamy cauliflower sauce works well with pasta for a carbonara-style sauce, or serve this dish alongside a vegan roast and Marmite roast potatoes for a big traditional dinner.

1 kg/2¼ lbs. Jerusalem artichokes

4 shallots

6 garlic cloves, left whole

½ cauliflower, cut into florets

1–2 tablespoons olive oil

1 teaspoon freshly ground white pepper

425 ml/1¾ cups almond milk or other vegan milk, plus extra if needed

2 tablespoons freshly squeezed lemon juice

½ teaspoon mustard powder

1 teaspoon onion powder

1 teaspoon salt

1 slice brown or rye bread, blitzed to rough breadcrumbs

3 tablespoons panko breadcrumbs

1 tablespoon freshly chopped marjoram or parsley (or ½ teaspoon dried)

2 tablespoons toasted hazelnuts, roughly chopped

SERVES 4–6

Peel the Jerusalem artichokes and slice into 5 mm/¼ inch-thick discs. Set aside in salted water to prevent them from discolouring.

Preheat the oven to 220°C (425°F) Gas 7.

Lay the shallots, garlic and cauliflower florets on a baking sheet and drizzle with half of the olive oil. Season with half of the pepper and toss slightly. Lay the Jerusalem artichoke slices on another baking sheet, drizzle with the rest of the olive oil and season with the remaining pepper. Place both baking sheets in the hot oven and roast for about 30 minutes until the cauliflower and artichokes are tender.

Transfer all the roasted vegetables, except the artichokes, to a food processor or blender, add the almond milk, lemon juice, mustard powder, onion powder and salt. Blitz until very smooth. Add more milk if necessary, to make a smooth, pourable sauce. Adjust the seasoning to taste if needed.

Layer the roast Jerusalem artichoke slices in a deep baking dish and then pour over the sauce. Sprinkle both types of breadcrumbs, the herbs and chopped hazelnuts over the top. Bake in the hot oven for about 20–30 minutes until golden on top and bubbling. Serve immediately.

SAVOY-WRAPPED QUINOA ROAST

This is another great vegan roast, very easy to prepare and looks impressive on the festive table. Perfect for a big roast dinner with family and friends, and it can be made with or without the vegan cheese (although the salty layer makes a flavoursome contrast to the filling). Serve with all the usual trimmings, of course.

1 tablespoon olive or other vegetable oil

1 red onion, diced into 5-mm/ ¼-inch pieces

½ courgette/zucchini, diced

1 carrot, diced

1 leek, finely sliced

5 chestnut mushrooms, diced

100 g/generous ½ cup quinoa or couscous

750 ml/3¼ cups vegetable stock

150 g/1¼ cups cashews

1 thick slice wholemeal/ whole-wheat or seeded bread

6 outer leaves from a Savoy cabbage, thick stalk ends trimmed

1 flax 'egg' (see page 138) or egg replacer

120 g/4½ oz. silken tofu

1 tablespoon each freshly chopped thyme and marjoram (or ½ teaspoon dried herbs)

120 g/4½ oz. vegan 'feta' or 'ricotta' (optional)

salt and freshly ground white pepper, to taste

2 lb./1 l. loaf pan, oiled

SERVES 6

Preheat the oven to 190°C (375°F) Gas 5.

Heat the olive oil in a pan and add the onion, courgette/zucchini, carrot, leek and mushrooms. Cook for 8–10 minutes until soft.

Simmer the quinoa in the vegetable stock for 4–5 minutes. Drain and set aside.

Toast the cashews in a dry frying pan/skillet for a few minutes, then bash (or blitz in a food processor) into small pieces. Avoid over-blitzing the nuts to a powder or you will lose the texture. Blitz the bread into crumbs. Blanch the cabbage leaves in boiling water for 2 minutes. Set aside.

Mix the vegetables, quinoa, nuts, breadcrumbs, flax 'egg' and tofu together in a bowl. Add the fresh or dried herbs and season to taste with salt and white pepper.

Line the oiled loaf pan with the cabbage leaves, using five large leaves to cover the bottom and sides and saving one leaf to seal the top. Half-fill the loaf pan with half of the veg mixture, firmly pushing it down with the back of a spoon. Crumble the vegan cheese (if using) over the filling, then add the remaining filling on top, again pushing down to create a firm shape.

Fold over the edges of the leaves to cover the top of the roast, and then place the last cabbage leaf on top and tuck it into the sides. Cover the pan with foil and place on a baking sheet. Bake in the preheated oven for 15 minutes, then turn over, foil-side down on the baking sheet, and bake for 10–15 minutes more.

Turn it the right way up again and remove the foil lid. Turn it out onto a board and serve in slices.

MARMITE & OLIVE OIL ROASTIES

There are great roast potatoes and then there are next level roast potatoes. And that includes these ones with their Marmite-y coating of joy! It is important to choose the right variety of potato to achieve the crispy exterior and fluffy interior. Most chefs and restaurants favour Maris Piper. Roughing up parboiled potatoes is also a key step in achieving the perfect roastie.

120 ml/½ cup olive oil, plus
    2 tablespoons for the Marmite/
    yeast extract paste
1 kg/2¼ lb. Maris Piper potatoes,
    or use King Edward or Rooster,
    peeled
35 g/1¼ oz. Marmite or similar
    yeast extract
1 bulb of garlic, cloves separated
    but unpeeled
3 or 4 sprigs of fresh rosemary

SERVES 5–6

Preheat the oven to 220°C (425°F) Gas 7.

Pour the olive oil into a deep baking pan and place in the preheated oven, until it's piping hot.

In a large pan, add the potatoes and cover with water, bring to the boil and then boil for 5 minutes. Drain the water using a colander or sieve/strainer, leaving the potatoes to stand for a few minutes so all the water evaporates. Then shake vigorously to rough up the edges of the potatoes. Place the potatoes back into the empty pan.

In a small bowl, add the Marmite or other yeast extract, add the extra 2 tablespoons of oil, then place in the microwave and heat on high for about 40–50 seconds to warm through slightly. Whisk together to make a runny paste. Pour this mixture over the potatoes and toss them so they are well coated.

Carefully remove the baking pan from the hot oven, then gently place the potatoes in the hot oil. They should sizzle as you do this.

Return the pan to the oven for 30 minutes. Remove and then carefully turn the potatoes over and scatter over the garlic and rosemary, then return to the oven for another 15–20 minutes until deep golden and crispy. Remove from the oven, and off drain any excess oil. Serve immediately.

GUINNESS-GLAZED BBQ MOCK HAM RIBS

This unapologetic mock meat recipe has all the texture and flavour of a robust meat-focussed dish. It can be served whole to be sliced at the table, like a ham, or sliced into chunky ribs on a sharing platter. It will impress your omnivore diners as well as mock meatloving vegans and vegetarians. Despite the long list of ingredients, it is quite straightforward to prepare. The leftovers can be used in a breakfast hash (see page 135) or thinly sliced for Boxing Day sandwiches. This recipe can be prepared in advance and will keep in the fridge for up to a week, or can be frozen before glazing.

FOR THE GLAZE

440 ml/15 fl. oz. can of Guinness

150 g/¾ cup soft brown sugar

1 teaspoon paprika

1 teaspoon freshly ground black pepper

2½ teaspoons corn or potato flour/starch

salt, to taste

FOR THE 'HAM RIB'
WET MIX

2 tablespoons olive or other vegetable oil

1 onion, finely chopped

4 sun-dried tomatoes (softened in olive oil), finely chopped

2 bay leaves

100 ml/⅓ cup plus 1 tablespoon passata/strained tomatoes

100 ml/⅓ cup plus 1 tablespoon good-quality vegetable stock

2 teaspoons salt

1 teaspoon caraway seeds

1 teaspoon hickory liquid smoke

2 tablespoons maple syrup

2 tablespoons soy sauce

DRY MIX

250 g/9 oz. wheat gluten

2 generous tablespoons chickpea/gram flour

2 tablespoons nutritional yeast

1 teaspoon onion powder

2 teaspoons garlic powder

2 teaspoons paprika

1 teaspoon dried sage

5 g/2 teaspoons dried dulse seaweed, soaked in cold water, drained and finely chopped

4 bay leaves

1 teaspoon coriander seeds and 1 teaspoon mustard seeds, roughly ground to a powder

ceramic or metal baking dish, approx. 25 x 15 cm/10 x 6 inches, lightly greased

SERVES 8

Preheat the oven to 180°C (350°F) Gas 4.

Put the bay leaves in the bottom of the prepared baking dish and scatter the ground coriander and mustard seeds over the bottom of the dish. Cut out a piece of greaseproof paper that will cover the top of the dish, and cut another piece of foil to the same size. Set aside.

To make the 'ham rib' wet mix, in a medium frying pan/skillet, add the oil and put over a medium heat. Add the chopped onion and fry gently for 12–15 minutes until translucent. Try not to colour it. Tip half of the cooked onion into another small pan and set aside.

Add the sun-dried tomatoes to the remaining half of the cooked onion, including any residual olive oil and the bay leaves, and fry gently for a few minutes. Then add all the remaining wet mix ingredients, and bring to a simmer again. Cook gently for 4–5 minutes, then discard the bay leaves. Set aside to cool.

Put all of the ingredients for the dry mix into a large bowl and add the cooled onion and tomato mixture from the frying pan/skillet. Mix well and knead the dough until it comes together. Press the dough into the bottom of the prepared baking dish making a thick layer that covers the bottom of the dish. Cover with the greaseproof paper and then the foil, wrapping over the edges for a snug fit.

Bake in the preheated oven for 1 hour. This will make a very chewy texture. Reduce the cooking time by 15 minutes if you prefer a softer texture, and reduce cooking time by a further 10 minutes if using a metal baking dish rather than ceramic.

Meanwhile, for the glaze, add the Guinness, sugar, paprika, pepper and salt to taste to the small pan with the reserved cooked onion. Place on a medium-high heat and bring to the boil. Reduce the heat and simmer for 30–40 minutes until reduced by a third. Mix the corn or potato flour/starch with a little cold water to make a paste, then mix into the glaze mixture to thicken. Simmer for a further 10 minutes until the glaze is sticky and well thickened. It should still have a pouring consistency.

Remove the 'ham' rib from the oven and remove the foil and paper. Generously coat with the glaze then carefully turn over – it should lift easily. Slather the top with more glaze and then return to the oven for another 8–10 minutes. You can also set aside after glazing and reheat in the oven for 10–15 minutes when you're ready to serve. Serve whole or sliced into 3 cm/1 inch wide ribs, drizzled in more of the warm glaze, and serve any extra on the side.

EASY CELEBRATION ROAST
WITH BEETROOT, APPLE & WALNUT STUFFING

This roast recipe was shaped by a classic recipe by Linda McCartney that I used to make for my veggie friends for their Christmas roasts in the early '90s. It would prove so popular that the omnivores would always be stealing slices. I've given this recipe a visual and flavour reboot with this delicious beetroot stuffing. The main roast is super simple to make with readily available ingredients, and is a great introductory recipe for home cooks who are new to making mock meat dishes.

1 tablespoon garlic powder

1 tablespoon onion powder

1 tablespoon dried mixed herbs

250 g/9 oz. dried vegan sausage mix, such as SosMix or Granovita

5 vegan burgers, mock meat variety, defrosted

125 g/4½ oz. frozen vegan mince, defrosted

4 tablespoons soy sauce

2 tablespoons gram/chickpea flour

FOR THE STUFFING

1 small brown onion, finely diced

2 tablespoons olive or other vegetable oil

8–10 slices brown bread

2 cooked beetroots/beets, grated

handful of fresh sage, roughly chopped

1 small eating apple, peeled and chopped into 5 mm pieces

small handful of walnuts, lightly toasted and roughly chopped

1 teaspoon salt

2 lb./1 litre loaf pan, lightly greased with 2 tablespoons oil

SERVES 8–10

Preheat the oven to 180°C (350°F) Gas 4.

Mix together the garlic and onion powders with the dried herbs, then tip into the prepared loaf pan. Gently shake to coat the oily base and sides with the herb mixture. Tip out any excess herbs and reserve for the stuffing bowl. Set aside.

Rehydrate the sausage mixture with approximately 400 ml/scant 1¾ cups boiling hot water (or according to packet instructions) and set aside for 10–15 minutes.

Place the burgers in a food processor and blend to make a thick paste. Place the paste in a large bowl and add the mince, soy sauce, the rehydrated sausage mixture and any of the remaining herb mixture. Using your hands, mix well, then scatter over the chickpea/gram flour and keep mixing until everything is well combined.

Lay half of the mixture into the loaf pan, pressing down with your hands to make a snug fit. Cover with greaseproof paper and a piece of foil, then place in the preheated oven and bake for 30 minutes. Remove from the oven and set aside to cool.

Meanwhile, make the stuffing. Put the diced onion into a small frying pan/skillet with the oil. Fry gently for 15–20 minutes until soft and translucent.

Put the bread into a food processor and blitz to make rough breadcrumbs. Tip into a large bowl. Add the cooked onion, grated beetroot/beet, sage, apple, walnuts and salt. Using a gloved hand or large spoon, combine to make a soft pliable mixture. Add a little water if needed.

Lay the stuffing mixture into the loaf pan, covering the first roasted layer with another layer approximately 2 cm/¾ inch thick. Press down firmly with your fingers. Do not fill the pan, the excess stuffing can be rolled into balls and baked on the side. Fill the pan with the remaining (uncooked) roast mixture, carefully covering the beetroot/beet stuffing so that it forms a layer in the middle of the roast. The roast mixture should fill the pan to the top. This can then be covered with greaseproof paper, then a layer of foil. Wrap tightly to make a snug cover and place in the fridge for a few hours or, even better, overnight.

When ready to bake, preheat the oven to 180°C (350°F) Gas 4.

Keep the roast wrapped, put it on a baking sheet and into the preheated oven for 1 hour 15 minutes. Remove from the oven, and take off the foil and paper covering. Carefully run a knife around the edge of the pan to loosen the roast. Return to the oven for another 15 minutes then remove and run the knife around the pan again. Gently turn the pan upside down onto a serving tray and lift the loaf pan off.

Serve the stuffed roast hot with gravy, extra stuffing, cranberry sauce and side dishes of roasted potatoes and vegetables.

ROASTED ONION GRAVY

2 tablespoons olive oil
3 red onions, thinly sliced
2 tablespoons plain/all-purpose flour
1 small glass of red wine (optional)
1 tablespoon soy sauce
1 teaspoon garlic powder
1 litre/quart Roasted Vegetable Stock
   (see page 141)
½ teaspoon freshly ground white
   pepper

In a heavy-bottomed pan, add the olive oil along with the sliced red onions. Fry over a medium-high heat for 12–15 minutes until well softened and browned. Add the flour and mix well. Cook for a minute or two, then add the wine (if using), soy sauce, garlic powder, stock and pepper. Bring to a simmer and cook over a low heat for 20–30 minutes. Taste and season with more soy sauce and pepper, if you like. Serve.

If preparing the gravy in advance, the red onions may turn blue in colour. This won't affect the flavour. Simply add 1 tablespoon of dark soy sauce and an additional 120 ml/½ cup of red wine before reheating, then serve immediately.

FESTIVE FINALES

BAKEORAMA'S SHOWSTOPPER LIMONCELLO 'NOG' TRIFLE

My talented pal Charlotte O'Toole created this retro-inspired recipe for our vegan Christmas pop-up one year and it was one of my favourite dishes from the banquet. Limoncello is a popular Italian post-dinner liqueur with a somewhat love/hate following. It can be substituted with another liqueur that you may prefer, such as Cointreau, or the alcohol can be omitted entirely. Replace the lemons for oranges if using Cointreau. There are several processes within this method and I recommend you make the curd in advance to reduce the preparation time. You can also replace the curd with your favourite jam but remember to omit the lemon zest from the sponge. The custard layer uses a crowd-pleasing ready-made custard formula, but the vegan custard can be made from scratch if you prefer. The trifle is best made the day before.

FOR THE LEMON CURD
3 tablespoons cornflour/cornstarch
juice of 5 large lemons
    (approximately 220 ml/1 cup)
pinch of salt
190 g/1 cup minus ½ tablespoon
    granulated sugar
60 ml/¼ cup unsweetened soy milk
80 g/3 oz. vegan butter

FOR THE SWISS ROLL SPONGE
(MAKES 2 ROLLS, APPROXIMATELY
16 SLICES)
475 ml/2 cups of unsweetened
    soy milk
300 g/1½ cups granulated sugar
2 teaspoons cider vinegar
235 ml/1 cup vegetable oil,
    such as sunflower or rapeseed
grated zest of 2 lemons
340 g/2½ cups of self-raising/
    rising flour

2 tablespoons cornflour/cornstarch
pinch of salt
1 teaspoon bicarbonate of/
    baking soda
1 teaspoon baking powder

FOR THE CUSTARD
75 g/scant ⅓ cup Bird's original
    custard powder (check the
    packaging, the original tub
    variety is vegan)
2 pints unsweetened soy milk
zest of ½ lime, finely chopped
70 g/⅓ cup plus 1 teaspoon
    granulated sugar
½ teaspoon vanilla paste or good
    quality vanilla extract

FOR THE CREAM
2 x 200 ml/8 oz. tubs Oatly or other
    plant-based crème fraîche
80 g/½ cup plus 1 tablespoon
    icing/confectioners' sugar
½ teaspoon vanilla paste or good
    quality vanilla essence

150–250 ml/⅔–1 cup plus
    1 tablespoon limoncello liqueur
    (optional)
2 tablespoons multi-coloured cake
    sprinkles
½ teaspoon edible glitter or other
    festive cake sprinkles (optional)

sterilized glass jar
2 Swiss roll/jelly roll pans, lightly oiled
    and lined with parchment paper

SERVES 12

To make the lemon curd, add the cornflour/cornstarch and 100 ml/
⅓ cup plus 1 tablespoon water to a small pan and mix well to make a
paste. Add the lemon juice, salt and sugar. Put the pan over a medium
heat and stir well until the sugar has dissolved and the curd is thickened
and smooth. Remove from the heat and add the soy milk and vegan
butter. Whisk well until smooth and glossy. Pour into a sterilized jar if
making ahead of time. The curd will keep in the fridge for up to 3 weeks.

Next prepare the Swiss roll sponge. Preheat the oven to 160°C (325°F)
Gas 3. In a large bowl, add the soy milk, sugar, vinegar, oil and zest.
Whisk together until the sugar has dissolved. Sift the flour, cornflour/
cornstarch, salt, bicarbonate of/baking soda and baking powder into
the bowl, then whisk together until the batter is smooth.

Divide the mixture between the two trays and bake in the preheated
oven for 20 minutes until slightly golden and cooked through.

Place two sheets of greaseproof paper on the table, the same length
as the baking trays.

Allow the sponge to cool slightly for a few minutes, then tip each
one onto each of the papers on the table. Peel off the lining paper,
which will now be on the top.

Spread each of the sponges with the lemon curd. Start to roll the
sponge up into a roll using the greaseproof to help curl and secure the
sponge until you have a long roll. Let it sit securely in the paper with
the join at the bottom until ready use.

Trim the end of each roll to neaten then cut into eight slices per roll.
Line the base of a large deep glass bowl with the slices and then arrange
decoratively around the edge so you can see a pattern on the outside.
Using large trifle bowl, you will have approximately half Swiss roll
leftover (perfect to use in Sunday Sundae page 108). Drizzle the slices
generously with limoncello if using.

Prepare the custard by mixing the powder with a little of the cold milk to make a paste. Add the remaining milk, lime zest, sugar and vanilla and place in a pan on a medium heat. Bring to simmer and whisk well to make a smooth custard. Remove from heat and cover with clingfilm/plastic wrap or greaseproof paper to prevent a skin forming on the custard. Set aside to cool.

Once fully cooled, pour the custard over the Swiss roll slices and then cover the bowl and set aside in the fridge to set.

Meanwhile prepare the sweetened cream by placing the Oatly crème fraiche in a large bowl. Sieve the icing/confectioners' sugar into the bowl and whisk well to combine.

Once the custard has cooled and set, billow the cream over the set custard. Cover the trifle and leave in the fridge overnight.

Just before serving, scatter the sprinkles over the top. Scatter with edible glitter too if you like.

SUNDAY SUNDAE

This 'leftovers' dessert is a great way to use up lots of the sweet stuff hanging around after the festive season. With memories of childhood Knickerbocker Glories and banana sundaes, you can lay the table with the various components for a 'build your own' dessert. You can substitute with whatever sweet leftovers you might have that seem to fit the bill. I usually end up making jelly/jello and a fruit compote to bring it all together.

1 packet of vegan jelly/jello, mango or raspberry make good combinations (most Indian grocers stock vegan jelly/jello as well as health food stores)

300–400 g/10½–14 oz. leftover cake (such as Swiss roll from trifle recipe on page 104)

150 g/1 cup frozen berries, such as raspberry, blueberries or mixed

1 teaspoon sugar

1 or 2 passion fruits

1 x 200 ml/8 oz. tub of Oatly crème fraîche, or ½ x 400 ml/ 14 fl. oz. can extra thick high quality coconut milk

40 g/¼ cup icing/confectioners' sugar, (add 20 g/2¼ tablespoons if using coconut milk)

handful of fresh, pitted cherries or handful fresh raspberries, halved

175 ml/¾ cup cardamom custard (see recipe on page 115) or substitute ½ x 250 ml/8 oz. tub of vegan vanilla ice-cream

3 or 4 vegan chocolate biscuits/ cookies, roughly broken

120 ml/½ cup canned sweetened mango purée

SERVES 4–6

Prepare the jelly/jello according to the packet instructions, pour into a large bowl and leave to set.

Cut the cake into bitesize chunks, approximately 2–3 cm/¾–1¼ inch cubes. Set aside.

Put the frozen berries into a small pan and add a teaspoon of sugar then heat gently until the fruit has broken down to make a thick compote. Set aside to cool.

Halve the passion fruits and scoop out the middle into another small bowl. Put the thick coconut milk (approx. 200 ml/1 cup) or Oatly vegan crème fraîche, if using, into a small bowl and sift in the icing/ confectioners' sugar into the bowl. Whisk together to make a thick sweetened cream. Put in the fridge until needed.

To build the sundae, put a couple of chunks of cake and some cherries or raspberries in a sundae glass a wide glass tumbler. Top with a big spoonful of jelly/jello and leftover custard or ice-cream, then add some broken biscuits/cookies followed by some berry compote, and some more custard. Repeat the layers, drizzling with a bit of mango purée and/or fruit compote here and there. Top with a layer of broken biscuits/cookies or cake crumbles and then a big spoonful of sweetened cream on the top. Drizzle over the fruit sauces and some passion fruit.

STICKY TOFFEE & RHUBARB PUDDING

I made this dessert one Sunday for my dairy-loving extended family and no-one realised they were eating a plant-powered pudding. The basic recipe is based on one I learned from one of Nigella's early books, which is an easy, no-mess sticky toffee pudding. The addition of rhubarb (or apples) brings a delicious tart edge alongside the sticky sweet sauce.

140 g/1 cup self-raising/self-rising flour

100 g/½ cup unrefined light brown sugar

1 tablespoon baking powder

pinch of salt

200 ml/scant 1 cup almond milk

85 g/3 oz. vegan margarine

1 flax 'egg' (see page 138) or egg replacer

scraped seeds from ½ vanilla pod/bean (or 1 teaspoon vanilla extract)

8 sticks of rhubarb, chopped into 2.5–5 cm/1–2 inch pieces

140 g/scant ¾ cup unrefined dark brown sugar

50 g/scant ½ cup pecans

TO SERVE
vegan ice-cream

deep baking dish, oiled

SERVES 6

Preheat the oven to 180°C (350°F) Gas 4.

In a large bowl, mix together the flour, light brown sugar, baking powder and salt.

Mix together the almond milk, margarine, flax 'egg' and vanilla seeds. Add to the dry ingredients and mix well to make a smooth batter.

Arrange the rhubarb in the prepared baking dish and pour the batter over the top of the fruit. Smooth across the fruit to ensure the rhubarb is well covered. In a small bowl, mix 250 ml/1 cup boiling water with the unrefined dark brown sugar until dissolved. Pour over the batter mixture, then scatter the pecans across the top. Bake in the preheated oven for about 40 minutes until the pudding has risen and is golden brown on top.

Use a big spoon to serve, making sure each bowl has an even mix of sponge, fruit and toffee sauce. Serve with vegan ice-cream.

SANTA'S VEGAN S'MORES

This recipe can be prepped in advance and the toppings can be added then grilled just before serving, so that it's warm and gooey. S'mores are an American campfire dessert where toasted marshmallows and dark chocolate squares are sandwiched between two graham crackers. This version makes a great sharing dessert for the feasting table, using the simplicity of a tray bake for an easy crowd-pleaser.

FOR THE BISCUIT BASE/CRUST

120 g/4½ oz. vegan digestive or oatie biscuits/graham crackers

120 g/4½ oz. vegan rich tea biscuits/cookies (such as McVities Tasties)

140 g/5 oz. vegan block margarine such as Stork, melted

3 tablespoons golden syrup

large pinch of salt

FOR THE CHOCOLATE FILLING

240 ml/1 cup unsweetened soy or other vegan milk

200 g/7 oz. dairy-free dark chocolate, approximately 70% cocoa, roughly chopped

60 g/2 oz. coconut oil, melted

2 tablespoons maple or agave syrup

large pinch sea salt

TOPPINGS

2 vegan digestive biscuits/graham crackers, broken into rough pieces

90 g/generous 3 oz. vegan marshmallows, such as Naked or Freedom Mallows

12 cherries, pitted and halved (preferably fresh but can substitute jarred), or substitute raspberries

25 g/generous ¾ oz. roughly chopped pistachios

deep baking sheet approximately 30 x 20 cm/12 x 8 inches, lined with greaseproof paper (trimmed to fit)

MAKES APPROXIMATELY 12–16 PIECES

To make the base/crust, blitz the biscuits/crackers in a food processor to make a crumb. Place in a large bowl with the remaining ingredients and mix well. The mixture should clump together when pressed. Put the mixture into the baking sheet and press down very firmly making an even layer using your fingers or the back of a spoon. Place the baking sheet in the fridge to set for 20–30 minutes.

To make the chocolate filling, heat the milk in a small pan over a low heat until almost boiling or heat in a bowl in the microwave. Add the chocolate and set aside for 5 minutes until the chocolate has almost completely melted. Stir in the melted coconut oil, syrup and salt with wooden spoon.

Using an electric or hand held mixer, whisk the chocolate filling to make a fluffy texture. Spread over the biscuit base/crust and return to the fridge to set for 20–30 minutes. You can freeze this dessert at this stage and then defrost and add the final toppings when ready to serve.

When ready to serve, top the tray bake with a scatter of marshmallows and the other toppings. Place under a hot grill/broiler for one or two minutes until the mallows start to brown and become gooey. Cut into squares and place on a platter and serve.

STOLLEN BREAD & BUTTER PUDDING
WITH CARDAMOM CUSTARD

This dessert has never failed to impress at the dinner table and is really quick to prepare. Of course you could also make your stollen from scratch. I have found most recipes are naturally vegan but I'm always short on time in the run up to Christmas, so I like to use a traditional ready-made one. You could easily halve this recipe if you had half a stollen leftover from the holiday season.

10–12 green cardamom pods (depending on how fat and fresh they are)

1200 ml/5 cups unsweetened oat, soy or other creamy vegan milk (I use Oatly Barista as it has great consistency for making vegan custard)

1–2 tablespoons white sugar, according to taste

½ vanilla pod or 1 tablespoon vanilla extract

750 g/26 oz. vegan German-style stollen loaf, 1-1.5 cm/⅓–½ inch sliced

½ x 220 g/8 oz. jar thick cut marmalade, preferably orange but any citrus will work well

3 heaped tablespoons cornflour/cornstarch

100 ml/scant ½ cup vegan cream, such as Oatly or soy cream

handful of sliced almonds

icing/confectioners' sugar, for dusting

ovenproof deep dish, approximately 5–7.5 cm/2–3 inches deep and 11 x 15 cm/4 x 5½ inches, lightly greased

SERVES 8–10

Pop open the cardamom pods and remove the sticky seeds inside. Grind to a powdery paste using a pestle and mortar or an electric grinder. You can also use the back of one spoon on top of another.

Put the ground cardamom seeds into a medium pan and put over a medium heat. Add 1 litre/4 cups of the vegan milk, sugar and vanilla extract, or the scraped vanilla seeds and pod shell if using. Bring to a simmer then turn off the heat. Let steep for 10–15 minutes. If making in advance you can prepare the entire dish without baking and it will keep in the fridge for several hours or even overnight.

Preheat the oven to 175°C (350°F) Gas 4.

Thickly spread each stollen slice on one side with the marmalade and layer into the prepared oven dish with the marmalade facing upwards, slightly overlapping each piece and filling the dish. Set aside.

Mix together the cornflour/cornstarch with a few tablespoons of cold water to make a paste. Remove the vanilla pod from the milk (or sieve the milk into a jug or bowl if some of your cardamom seeds were a little unbroken). Then add the cornflour/cornstarch mixture to the milk, along with 100 ml/⅓ cup plus 1 tablespoon vegan cream whisk together well and heat gently until thickened. Pour approximately 750 ml/3¼ cups of the custard mixture over the stollen slices, so they are well covered. Scatter with almond slices. Set aside the remaining custard to reheat in a small pan, whisking until thick and creamy. Bake the pudding in the preheated oven for 50 minutes until deep golden brown and bubbling.

Dust with icing/confectioners' sugar just before serving. Serve the extra custard alongside the baked pudding.

PLUM & PISTACHIO CRUMBLE
WITH STAR ANISE CUSTARD

There's nothing that says comfort food quite like a crumble. A good crumble recipe is easy to make and adaptable to any season. The addition of pistachios always feels a little luxurious, and the star anise custard is a recipe you'll want to use again as it pairs well with many fruit puddings.

2 kg/4½ lb. plums, washed and
   stoned/pitted, halved (or
   quartered if they are very large)
6 Indonesian long peppercorns
   (or 6 cloves)
2 tablespoons unrefined brown
   sugar
1 teaspoon ground cinnamon

FOR THE CRUMBLE
250 g/scant 2 cups plain/
   all-purpose flour
180 g/6½ oz. vegetable margarine
120 g/1¼ cups jumbo oats
100 g/½ cup unrefined brown sugar
80 g/¾ cup pistachios, roughly
   chopped

FOR THE CUSTARD
570 ml/scant 2½ cups soy or
   almond milk, plus a splash extra
3–4 star anise, roughly ground so
   that the seeds are crushed slightly
1 vanilla pod/bean, split
1½ tablespoons cornflour/
   cornstarch
about 120 ml/½ cup soy or almond
   cream, to taste
about 2 tablespoons unrefined
   light brown sugar, to taste

SERVES 6

Preheat the oven to 190°C (375°F) Gas 5.

Layer the plums and Indonesian peppercorns into a deep baking dish, and sprinkle with the sugar and cinnamon powder.

To make the crumble, sift the flour into a large bowl and add the margarine. Rub together with your finger tips to make a breadcrumb-like texture, then add the oats, sugar and pistachios. Mix well and layer on top of the plums. Bake in the preheated oven for 35–45 minutes until bubbling and the crumble is golden brown.

To make the custard, bring the milk to a gentle boil together with the star anise. Scrape in the seeds from the vanilla pod/bean and then add the scraped pod/bean as well. Simmer gently for 5 minutes, then remove from the heat and set aside for 15–20 minutes while the flavours infuse.

Mix together the cornflour/cornstarch with the extra splash of cold milk to make a paste. Strain the infused milk to remove any large bits. Whisk the cornflour/cornstarch paste into the warm milk and return to the heat. Bring to a simmer again for a few minutes. Add the almond cream and sugar to taste. Remove from the heat. If not using immediately, cover the surface with clingfilm/plastic wrap to stop a skin forming. Serve the crumble in bowls with warm custard.

PANNA COTTA
WITH CANDIED KUMQUATS

Candied fruit is a common festive treat in Mediterranean Europe and seasonal kumquats are the perfect size and shape for a dessert, and will keep for several months too. The panna cotta is a great dessert – light and creamy and satisfying all at the same time. This makes a perfect ending to any dinner party. Mainly because it's already prepared and no-one wants to be in the kitchen at this point in the evening. My MasterChef buddy Sara often serves perfectly formed sable biscuits alongside this Italian classic. But Oreos also work brilliantly too!

FOR THE CANDIED KUMQUATS
250 ml/1 cup water
300 g/1½ cups granulated sugar
½ vanilla pod/bean, halved
    lengthways and seeds scraped
500 g/1 lb. 2 oz. kumquats

FOR THE PANNA COTTA
2 tablespoons cornflour/cornstarch
700 ml/scant 3 cups soy milk
80 g/5½ tablespoons caster/
    granulated sugar
9 g/1 tablespoon agar agar
250 ml/1 cup orange juice

6–7 small 120–150 ml/4–5 fl. oz.
    panna cotta moulds or cups

MAKES 6–7

To make the candied kumquats, in a small saucepan, heat the water, sugar, vanilla seeds and the scraped pod/bean, and bring to a simmer. Add the kumquats, reduce the heat and simmer for 15–20 minutes until the kumquats are tender and soft, and the syrup is thick enough to coat a spoon. Set aside.

For the panna cotta, dissolve the cornflour/cornstarch in 2–3 tablespoons of the milk, and set aside. Mix the remaining milk with the sugar, agar agar and orange juice in a small pan. Bring to a simmer, and cook for 6 minutes. Add the cornflour/cornstarch mixture and cook for a further 3–4 minutes. Strain through a fine sieve/strainer into 6 or 7 small cups or moulds. Leave to cool for 15 minutes, then set aside in the fridge for at least an hour.

When ready to serve, place a serving plate on to of the mould and quickly flip over. The mould might need a shake to release the panna cotta. If it seems stuck, gently warm the outside of the mould with a hot, damp cloth. Just before serving, spoon two or three of the candied kumquats on top of the dessert, and drizzle some of the leftover sauce over the top.

PINEAPPLE & CARDAMOM UPSIDE-DOWN CAKE

I was about 8 years old when I made my very first pineapple upside-down cake. I followed the recipe from one of my mum's '70s cookery books. I even made her buy the glacé/candied cherries so it would look like the picture. This is like a grown-up version of those childhood memories. I created this recipe following my stint in the pastry kitchen at Benares, Atul Kochher's famous Mayfair restaurant. As well as creating exquisite Indian food, the team introduced me to the joy of Asian-inspired desserts and pastries. When I admitted I was less keen on traditional Indian desserts, they taught me to take something you love and find an Asian flavour that works well with it. If you're not a cake eater, you could simply poach the pineapple with the cardamom and serve with a scoop of vegan ice-cream. Either way, pineapple and cardamom is a delicious combo however you serve it. It's important to use the right amount of cardamom, as it can taste soapy if you add too much.

1 fresh pineapple (or 300 g/10½ oz. canned pineapple), cut into rings or pieces

1½ tablespoons coconut oil

160 g/generous ¾ cup caster/superfine sugar

225 g/1¾ cups self-raising/self-rising flour

125 g/4 oz. vegan margarine

80 ml/⅓ cup vegan or soy milk

2 flax 'eggs' (see page 138) or egg replacer

1 teaspoon baking powder

1 teaspoon pure vanilla extract

10 green cardamoms, shelled and seeds removed

20-cm/8-inch cake pan, base-lined with greaseproof paper

SERVES 6–8

Preheat the oven to 170°C (325°F) Gas 3.

Soften the coconut oil and rub 20 g/1½ tablespoons of the sugar into it. Rub this mixture around the bottom of the lined cake pan and halfway up the sides. Place the pineapple slices across the bottom of the lined cake pan. Set aside.

Grind the cardamom seeds to a powder with a pestle and mortar. Then sift the ground cardamom into a bowl along with the remaining ingredients and whisk together with an electric hand-held whisk.

Pour the mixture into the cake pan and place in the preheated oven for 50–60 minutes, until the cake is evenly risen and a skewer inserted into the centre of the cake comes out clean.

Allow the cake to cool in the pan for 15 minutes before turning out onto a wire rack to cool completely.

PEAR & FRANGIPANE TART

Frangipane tarts are one of my go-to vegan desserts, because they don't have to be made with eggs. It feels indulgent and pairs so well with different fruits – the combinations are fairly endless and you can adapt to the different seasons. I sometimes make this tart with greengages, a highly regarded sweet plum, but they're not easy to find in the UK, whereas pears are readily available everywhere.

350 g/12 oz. vegan pastry
   (see page 52)
flour, for dusting
4 large pears
freshly squeezed lemon juice
150 g/5½ oz. vegan margarine or
   coconut butter, cut into pieces
150 g/¾ cup granulated sugar
180 g/1¾ cups ground almonds
50 g/6 tablespoons plain/
   all-purpose flour
½ teaspoon ground cinnamon
small pinch of salt
160 ml/⅔ cup plain almond milk
½ vanilla pod/bean, halved
   lengthways and seeds scraped
   (or 2 teaspoons pure vanilla extract)
½ teaspoon almond extract
60 g/scant 3 tablespoons apricot
   jam/jelly
icing/confectioners' sugar,
   for dusting
vegan vanilla ice-cream or almond
   cream, to serve

large 20–24-cm/8–10-inch tart pan
   or four 8–10-cm/3–4-inch individual
   tart pans, greased with vegan
   margarine or butter
baking beans

SERVES 4

Preheat the oven to 160°C (325°F) Gas 3.

Prepare the pastry base, by rolling out the pastry on a well-floured surface to 3–4 mm/⅛ inch thickness. Line the greased tart pan(s) with the shortcrust pastry, ensuring the pastry is pushed into the corners or fluted edge and allowing the pastry to overhang the top edge of the pan. Cover the pastry with baking parchment, and then add the baking beans to cover the tart base. If you have time, rest this pastry case in the fridge for 20 minutes.

Bake in the preheated oven for 25–30 minutes until the pastry is almost cooked with little colour. Take the tart base out of the oven and remove the beans and paper. Place back in the oven, uncovered, for 10 minutes. Remove and set aside ready to fill.

Peel the pears, slice in half and remove the cores. Set aside in a bowl of lemon water to stop them browning.

In a food processor, blitz together the margarine, sugar, ground almonds, flour, ground cinnamon and salt. Continue to pulse and then slowly pour in the almond milk, along with vanilla seeds (or extract if using) and almond extract. Mix to form a thick batter. Spread the almond mixture into the tart case. Slice each pear half with crossways cuts to create a fan. Gently press each pear fan into the mixture.

Bake the tart in the preheated oven for 30–40 minutes until the top is golden brown, then move the tart onto a cooling rack and cool for 20 minutes. In a small pan, melt the jam for a few minutes over medium heat, stirring often. Alternatively melt in a microwave for a minute or two. It should be liquid enough to brush on top of the pie. Brush the top of the tart and pears with the melted jam. Leave the tart to cool for another hour or so. Dust with icing/confectioners' sugar and serve with a scoop of vanilla ice-cream or some almond cream.

CHAI-SPICED RICE PUDDING
WITH GINGER COOKIES

This Indian twist on the beloved childhood pudding makes a delicious dessert for all the family. You can also use the spice mix to make Indian masala tea.

FOR THE CHAI SPICE MIX

2 teaspoons ground ginger (use slices of fresh if you are making tea)

¼ teaspoon ground cinnamon (use 1 large piece of cassia bark or cinnamon stick for tea)

4–5 green cardamom pods, seeds removed and crushed

1 teaspoon ground fennel (use fennel seeds if making tea)

pinch of ground black pepper

2 cloves (optional)

FOR THE PUDDING

100 g/3½ oz. Arborio rice

seeds from 1 vanilla pod/bean

400-ml/14-oz. can coconut milk

350 ml/1½ cups almond, soy, oat or rice milk, plus extra if needed

150 ml/⅔ cup almond or soy cream, plus extra if needed

pinch of freshly grated nutmeg

3 tablespoons brown sugar

FOR THE GINGER BISCUITS/COOKIES

150 g/generous 1 cup self-raising/self-rising flour, plus extra if needed

½ teaspoon bicarbonate of soda/baking soda

2 teaspoons ground ginger

40 g/1½ oz. stem ginger, finely chopped

1 teaspoon ground cinnamon

2 teaspoons caster/superfine sugar

50 g/2 oz. vegan margarine

2 tablespoons golden/light corn syrup

FOR THE MANGO COULIS

1 ripe mango, peeled, stone/pit removed and flesh cubed

TO SERVE

toasted pistachios

2 baking sheets, oiled

SERVES 4–6

Preheat the oven to 190°C (375°F) Gas 5.

Gently toast all the spices for the chai spice mix in a dry frying pan/skillet until the aroma is released.

To make the pudding, place the rice, the seeds of the vanilla pod/bean, the coconut milk, almond milk, almond cream and nutmeg in a large, deep pan. Bring to a gentle boil and add the toasted spices. Simmer for 40–45 minutes, stirring occasionally, adding more cream or milk if needed – the rice should retain a little bite. Sweeten with the sugar.

Meanwhile, make the biscuits/cookies. Mix all the dry ingredients together in a bowl. In a small pan, gently melt the margarine and syrup together. Pour the melted mixture into the bowl and mix well with the dry ingredients to form a soft and pliable dough. Add more flour if necessary, so that the dough is not too sticky. Roll the dough into small balls.

Flatten the dough balls slightly and place onto the oiled baking sheets, leaving space between each as the mixture will spread as it cooks. Bake in the preheated oven for 10–15 minutes, or until golden. Allow to firm up slightly on the baking sheets, then transfer to a wire rack to cool completely.

For the coulis, put the mango pieces into a small pan with a splash of water and heat gently until very soft. Blend in a food processor or push through a sieve/strainer to make a smooth coulis.

To serve, fill a ramekin with rice pudding and add a swirl of mango coulis. Serve with ginger cookies on the side and sprinkle with the toasted pistachios.

LOVE
YOUR
LEFTOVERS

FESTIVE PASTIES

This recipe makes the most of all those leftover winter veggies, all wrapped up in this
Cornish-style pasty. You can use whatever leftovers you have in the fridge, and even make
miniature pasties for a sharing platter if you like. I like to keep the spicing simple with just
salt and pepper, especially when adding leftover stuffing or nut roast. And a big dollop of
cranberry sauce of course.

FOR THE DOUGH

500 g/3¾ cups strong/bread flour,
    plus extra for dusting/rolling
120 g/4 oz. vegetable suet
25 g/1¾ tablespoons butter
    or margarine
½ teaspoon salt

FOR THE FILLING

2 large handfuls of vegetable
    leftovers such as roast potatoes,
    mash, peas and roasted root
    vegetables
1 large slice or handful of vegan
    or nut roast leftovers
1 large handful of stuffing leftovers
    (approximately 3 tablespoons)
1 teaspoon salt
1 teaspoon ground white pepper
4 generous tablespoons cranberry
    sauce
2 tablespoons vegan butter
    or margarine
1 teaspoon freshly ground
    black pepper
3 tablespoons soy milk and
    1 teaspoon salt, for glazing
vegetable oil, for frying

MAKES 4 LARGE OR
6 MEDIUM SIZED PASTIES

Mix all of the dough ingredients together to make a breadcrumb
texture. Add 175 ml/¾ cup water and knead well until dough is soft
and pliable. Add a little more water if needed. Leave to rest in the
fridge for at least an hour.

Preheat the oven to 170°C (325°F) Gas 3.

Dice the leftovers into 2 cm/¾ inch pieces. Mix the leftovers
together in a bowl and season with salt and white pepper.

Divide the dough into 4 or 6 equal-sized pieces. Roll out the
dough onto a floured surface into circle. Milk wash the pastry edges.

Fill half of the circle with the leftovers mixture, add a spoonful of
cranberry sauce (to taste) in the centre then add a knob of margarine
and a sprinkle of black pepper over top, then fold over the dough,
to make a large half moon shape.

Crimp the edges, using one forefinger to fold over the underneath
edge and pressing down on the top with the other forefinger (so the
underside layer is folded over with the top layer, then crimped into
place). This will make the crust extra thick like a traditional Cornish
pasty. Brush generously with salted milk wash.

Bake in the preheated oven for 30–40 minutes until golden
brown. Serve warm with extra cranberry sauce if you like.

BUBBLE & SQUEAK PARATHAS

This is one of my favourite leftovers recipes, guaranteed to get everyone eating the vegetables they normally avoid on their Christmas plate — yes sprouts I'm talking to you! Leftover vegetables make the best paratha stuffing at any time of the year, but there's something very lovely about this Indo-Euro recipe. Most northern Europeans have a version of hash using leftover veg, especially potatoes and greens. In our house it was colcannon, but bubble & squeak was the Christmas version where pretty much anything could go into the hash.

FOR THE DOUGH

900 g/32 oz. wholemeal chapatti (atta) flour

3 tablespoons olive oil

½ tablespoon salt

½ tablespoon ajwain (caraway) seeds

400–450 ml/14–15 fl. oz. warm water

FOR THE FILLING

This will make approximately 16 heaped tablespoons of chopped assorted leftover veg, but any combination will work, even leftover stuffing:

4 parsnips, 6 Brussels sprouts, 2 tablespoons red cabbage, 4 roast potatoes, 3 tablespoons mash potato, 1 tablespoon peas

1 medium-large brown onion, finely diced

handful fresh coriander/cilantro, roughly chopped

1 red chilli/chile, finely chopped (optional)

½ teaspoon amchoor (green mango powder) or add juice of ½ lemon (approximately 2 tablespoons)

oil for frying, such as rapeseed or coconut

MAKES 10–12 STUFFED PARATHAS

The filling for these can include whatever cooked vegetables you have leftover (or grate any raw veg like carrot or cauliflower), and I often serve them with a really simple dhal, so the paratha gets to be the star of the show. A great winter warmer for a cozy evening by the fire.

Add all the dough ingredients to a large bowl or mixer, and add 200 ml/1 cup water. Combine well, adding more water as needed, mixing until it becomes a soft dough. Knead or mix the dough for 8–10 minutes until soft and pliable. Cover the dough in a bowl and leave to rest for an hour at room temperature.

Dice all the leftover vegetables. Mix the leftover vegetables together in a bowl, adding the finely diced onion (or any other raw grated veg), coriander/cilantro, chilli/chile, amchoor or lemon juice if using. If I am serving with a spicy dhal, I don't add any extra chilli/chile to the paratha. Season the mixture with salt if needed.

Divide the dough into 10–12 pieces, rolling into small balls. Lightly flour the work surface and roll out the paratha to approximately 18 cm/ 7 inch wide circle. Place 4–5 generous tablespoonfuls of veg mix in the centre and spread out slightly to halfway across the circle. Fold in the sides, bringing outer edge to centre and covering the filling. Make 5 or 6 folds, bringing outer edge inwards to centre, moving around the circle to make a stuffed pentagon or polygon shape. The filling should be well covered and the folds overlapping slightly.

Now gently roll out the paratha again, flattening the disc and gently pushing out any air bubbles. Roll out to approximately 2 cm/¾ inch thickness. Some of the vegetables may poke through here and there. Gently set aside, layering with greaseproof paper and complete stuffing the remaining parathas.

Heat a large flat frying pan/skillet on high, adding a tablespoon of oil. Gently lay a paratha in the hot oil and turn down heat to medium high. Cook for 3–4 minutes on each side, turning carefully until nicely browned on both sides and the dough is cooked through. Place the cooked paratha in a warm oven while cooking the remaining breads. They can also be cooled and refrigerated for up to 3 days. Then reheated later on baking sheets in a warm oven at 175˚C (350˚F) Gas 4.

CROSTINI SHARING PLATTER

This is the easiest sharing platter of all in my opinion, because you can prepare both the crostini and the toppings in advance. The broad bean purée and the mushroom pates can also be frozen, so it's worth picking up a catering size box of fresh mushrooms to make a large batch of the pate, then freeze into smaller portions for later use. Choose a good quality sourdough baguette and once the slices are baked and cooled, you can store in an airtight container to use as needed.

1 sourdough baguette, sliced on an
    angle approximately 1 cm/³⁄₈ inch
    thick
1 recipe aubergine/eggplant jeow
    (see page 10)
mushroom pate (see page 87)
broad bean purée (see page 14)
fresh coriander/cilantro leaves,
    to serve
fresh mint leaves, to serve
fresh thyme, to serve

Preheat the oven to 120°C (250°F) Gas ½.

Slice the baguette at an angle with approximately 1 cm/³⁄₈ inch width. Put the baguette slices onto a baking sheet and bake in the preheated oven for 20–30 minutes until crisp but not browned. Remove the crostini from the oven and allow to cool. The crostinis can be kept in an airtight container until ready to use.

Spread the crostini slices with the aubergine/eggplant jeow, mushroom pate and/or broad bean purée. Then top with some fresh herbs; coriander/cilantro for the aubergine/eggplant jeow, mint for the broad bean purée and fresh thyme or parsley for the mushroom pate. Serve immediately.

CORNED BEEFY HASH

This recipe uses the same roast recipe from the Wellington (see page 87), but simply changes the dry rub mixture, and the roasting pan ingredients have been rebooted with the addition of some beloved Guinness. You can make a hash using whatever leftovers you have, including roasted veg, mashed veg and any diced mock meat or vegan roast.

Wellington roast recipe
(see page 87)
2 large potatoes, peeled
and cubed
1 tablespoon olive oil,
plus extra for drizzling
1 onion, thickly sliced
1 green (bell) pepper,
cored, deseeded and
thickly diced
2 tablespoons
Henderson's Relish or
vegan Worcestershire
sauce
½ teaspoon freshly
ground black pepper
½–1 teaspoon sea salt,
to taste

FOR THE DRY RUB
2 teaspoons black
mustard seeds
1 teaspoon freshly
ground black pepper
1 teaspoon ground
allspice
½ teaspoon ground
ginger
pinch of ground
cinnamon

FOR THE ROASTING PAN
450 ml/scant 2 cups
good-quality vegetable
stock
1 tablespoon sea salt
1 onion, quartered, skin
left on
1 large can of Guinness
(which is vegan in UK
and Eire) or other dark
stout
1 teaspoon dried juniper
berries
1 tablespoon olive
or vegetable oil
½ teaspoon whole cloves

*medium muslin/cheesecloth
sheet, approx. 40.5 cm/
16 inches square,
lightly oiled*
twine, for tying

SERVES 4

Preheat the oven to 180°C (350°F) Gas 4. Add all the roasting pan ingredients into a large, deep roasting pan and set aside.

Mix together the dry rub ingredients and scatter on the work surface. Roll the mock meat dough in the dry rub, then lay on the lightly oiled muslin/cheesecloth and roll so the roast is snugly wrapped in the cloth. Tie each end with twine. Tie further loops around the roast to ensure it is fairly tightly wrapped and secure. Lay the roast in the prepared roasting pan, cover the pan with foil and place in the preheated oven for 2 hours. Turn once halfway through cooking. Remove the foil cover and return to the oven for a further 30–40 minutes, then remove and set aside to cool slightly for about 1 hour. Then remove the muslin/cheesecloth.

Slice the roast into four big pieces and then, using a knife or your hands, slice or tear the roast pieces into large chunks. You will only need 400 g/14 oz. of the roasted chunks for this dish to serve 4. The remaining roast can be frozen for several months.

Place a medium pan half-filled with water over a high heat. Bring to the boil and add the potatoes. Boil for about 8–10 minutes until just softening, then drain and set aside.

In a large frying pan/skillet, add the olive oil and then the onion and (bell) pepper. Fry for 2–3 minutes, then add the potatoes and fry for another 8–10 minutes until lightly browned. Season. Add the roasted chunks and mix well, frying on a high heat. Finally, drizzle with a little olive oil, mix well and serve immediately with Henderson's Relish on the side.

NEXT-DAY NOODLE SOUP

This is a delicious light soup. Perfect for using up leftovers and post-indulgent festive feasting. Mung bean or thread noodles (sometimes also called glass or cellophane noodles) are extremely nutritious, but you could also use any noodles you like such as rice or yellow noodles. The broth is packed with fragrant South East Asian flavours.

600 g/21 oz. mung bean noodles or rice vermicelli noodles
1 tablespoon toasted sesame oil
1 tablespoon vegetable oil
8 garlic cloves, crushed
2 sticks of lemongrass, crushed and finely chopped
1 tablespoon finely chopped ginger
800 ml/28 fl. oz. vegetable stock or water
2 tablespoons light soy sauce or tamari
1 teaspoon soft brown sugar
150 g/5½ oz. leftover root veg, such as carrot, parsnip, swede, beetroot/beets and turnip, diced
150 g/5½ oz. leftover shredded cabbage (preferably red and green)

handful of leftover Brussels sprouts, quartered (optional)
freshly squeezed juice of 1 lime

TO SERVE
2 spring onions/scallions, sliced (including the green parts)
handful of fresh coriander/cilantro
2–3 red chillies/chiles, finely sliced (optional)
Thai chilli/chili jam or sambal (optional)
lime quarters (optional)

SERVES 3–4

Put the noodles in a large bowl and cover with boiling water. Leave for 4–5 minutes until the noodles are soft. Rinse, drain and set aside.

Heat the sesame and vegetable oils in a large pan over a medium heat and cook the garlic for 10–15 minutes, until golden brown. Add the lemongrass and ginger and fry gently for a further 5–10 minutes.

Add the vegetable stock or water and bring to the boil. Add the soy sauce and sugar, bring back to the boil, then simmer for 5 minutes.

If using raw leftover vegetables, add the diced root veg and simmer gently for 6–8 minutes until just cooked. Then add two thirds of the shredded cabbage and Brussels sprouts. Bring back to the boil then remove from the heat immediately. If using cooked leftover vegetables, add at the same time as the cabbage, bringing to a sustained simmer, then remove from the heat.

Put the drained softened noodles into the pan, mix well and add the lime juice. Add a little more boiling water to pan if needed. The broth should generously cover all the veg and noodles. Then divide the noodles and vegetable broth between the bowls. Top the bowl of noodle soup with some of the remaining raw shredded cabbage (if using raw), spring onions/scallions, coriander/cilantro leaves and fresh chillies/chiles, if using. Serve with lime wedges and chilli/chili jam or sambal on the side if you like.

BASIC RECIPES

CASHEW CREAM

Making your own vegan cream is as easy
as buying a carton from the shop, and the
nutritional value will be far greater. To save
on costs, buy unsalted raw cashews in large
bags from an Indian grocer. The cream will
keep for 5 days in the fridge.

140 g/scant 1¼ cups raw cashews
350 ml/1½ cups filtered water,
    plus extra for soaking
½ teaspoon salt

MAKES 500 ML/2 CUPS

Soak the raw cashews in filtered water for 2–3
hours. Drain and rinse. Add the rinsed nuts to the
filtered water and salt, and blitz in a food processor
or blender until completely smooth. Add more
water to achieve the required consistency.

AQUAFABA 'EGG'

This is simply chickpea water – the liquid from
a can of chickpeas – that has taken on some
of the protein from the chickpeas and forms an
egg-white-like substitute. Some cooks use it to
make meringue, but it's highly unstable and you
have to add an excessive amount of sugar to
cover the flavour of chickpeas. However, it does
make an excellent ingredient in savoury food.

The best aquafaba is where the water is
drained and then boiled until it is reduced by
half. The reduced liquid should then be chilled,
where it will become quite gelatinous.

FLAX 'EGG'

There are a number of techniques for making
egg replacements in vegan cooking. My personal
favourite is the flax 'egg'. For a start, it's highly
nutritious as it uses ground linseeds/flaxseeds
which are full of essential omega-3 and omega-6
fatty acids. I use plain linseeds/flaxseeds, but
you can use the hulled version if you prefer.
It makes little difference, other than cost, as
the seeds are ground to a paste anyway.

You will need a spice or coffee grinder, or
the ubiquitous Nutribullet. A good grinder is
an essential piece of equipment for grinding
any seeds to a consistent powder. Flax 'eggs'
will keep for up to 3 days in the fridge. You may
find you need to add more water to the mixture
after a day or two, as it tends to thicken further
as time goes on.

1 tablespoon freshly ground
    linseeds/flaxseeds
3 tablespoons filtered water

MAKES 1 EGG REPLACER

To make one egg, mix together the freshly ground
linseeds/flaxseeds and water. Place in the fridge
for about 20–30 minutes and the mixture will
become gel-like and ready to use as an egg
substitute. To save time, I make four or five times
this quantity as it will keep in the fridge for a few
days. You can also substitute chia seeds if you like.

EASY VEGAN MAYONNAISE

Aquafaba, or chickpea water, has been a
revelation for me. Basically the water in that
can of chickpeas has enough protein in it that
it can be wildly transformed. Aquafaba mayo is
very easy to make and much more cost-effective
than the expensive shop-bought stuff.

2 small garlic cloves, crushed
1 tablespoon lemon juice
2 teaspoons Dijon mustard
3 tablespoons liquid from a can
   of chickpeas, plus 12 whole
   chickpeas
120 ml/½ cup vegetable oil
60 ml/¼ cup extra virgin olive oil
½ teaspoon salt
½ teaspoon black pepper

MAKES 250 ML/1 CUP

Using a food processor or stick blender, blitz
the garlic, lemon juice, mustard, chickpea liquid
and chickpeas until completely smooth. With the
blender running, slowly add the vegetable oil until
the mixture becomes smooth and creamy.

Transfer to a bowl, and whisk constantly while
slowly pouring in the olive oil. Season with salt and
pepper. Transfer to clean jar or container. The mayo
will keep for a week in the fridge.

VEGAN FISH SAUCE

Make a batch of this fish sauce and keep it in
the fridge for your vegan cooking. It's a great
staple seasoning and is used in a host of dishes,
marinades and dipping sauces including the
Rice Paper Rolls (see page 17) and Sticky BBQ
Skewers (see page 13). The sauce can be kept
in the fridge for several months.

50 g/1¾ oz. dried seaweed
   (such as laver, dulse or arame),
   cut into small strips
500 ml/2 cups plus 2 tablespoons
   light soy sauce or tamari
8 black peppercorns
2 garlic cloves, peeled
1 dried Chinese or shiitake
   mushroom

MAKES 250 ML/1 CUP

Add 500 ml/2 cups plus 2 tablespoons of water to
a medium pan and add the dried seaweed. Bring
to the boil and then simmer for 30–40 minutes
until the water has reduced by more than half.
Leave to stand for an hour. Strain the mixture,
reserving the liquid in another bowl. Rinse the
pan and add the soy sauce or tamari, then add the
peppercorns, garlic and dried mushroom. Bring to
a simmer, and add the seaweed reduction. Simmer
for 30–40 minutes until the mixture has reduced to
less than half again. Strain and store in a sterilized
glass bottle in the fridge until needed.

MOCK CHKN PIECES

This is a great recipe for a flavourful chicken substitute that can be made into bite-sized pieces or adapted to make escalopes, nuggets or wings.

200 g/7 oz. vital wheat gluten
2 tablespoons nutritional yeast
1 tablespoon onion powder
1 teaspoon Herbamare seasoning
½ teaspoon sea salt
½ teaspoon dried thyme
½ teaspoon dried marjoram
35 ml/2 tablespoons tahini
150 ml/ cup vegetable stock

FOR THE BRAISING PAN
1–1.5 litres/1 quart–6 cups plus
    4 tablespoons vegetable stock
4 garlic cloves, slightly smashed
handful of fresh herbs, such as
    rosemary and/or thyme

flour, for dusting

MAKES APPROX. 4 ESCALOPES/
20 WINGS

To prepare the mock chkn, mix together the dry ingredients in a medium bowl. In a jug/pitcher, mix together the tahini and stock. Make a well in the centre of the bowl, and pour in two thirds of the stock mixture. Combine the ingredients to make a stiff dough, adding more of the stock mixture as needed. The dough should be nice and firm. Knead well for a minute. Leave to rest for 5–10 minutes.

Preheat the oven to 170°C (325°F) Gas 4. Prepare a braising pan by adding all the ingredients into a deep oven pan and place on middle shelf in the preheated oven for 10–15 minutes.

Place the dough on a well-floured surface and cut into 4 pieces. Roll each piece into a large sausage shape.

Remove the braising pan from the oven and place the mock chkn into the pan. Cover with foil and bake in the preheated oven for 40 minutes. Remove the foil and then bake, uncovered, for a further 10–20 minutes (depending on size of the chkn pieces). Set the cooked mock chkn pieces on paper towels to drain.

The pieces can be cooled and chopped into bite-sized pieces to use in other recipes as a substitute for chicken. These pieces can also be minced/ground using a food processor. The minced/ground chkn can then be frozen for later use.

ROASTED VEGETABLE STOCK

This roasted stock will bring an intense and robust flavour to lots of recipes, especially soups and stews. It will keep in the fridge for a week or it can be frozen.

1 celery bunch, roughly chopped

2 large fennel bulbs, roughly chopped

8 carrots, peeled and thickly sliced

3 onions, skin on, quartered

2 beef/beefsteak tomatoes, quartered

3 tablespoons olive oil

480 ml/2 cups red wine, such as Syrah

5 litres/5¼ quarts water

400-g/14-oz. can cannellini or white beans, rinsed

2 bay leaves

2-cm/¾-inch sprig of tender rosemary

30 g/1 oz. dried porcini mushrooms or other dried mushrooms

1 teaspoon peppercorns

1 teaspoon salt

MAKES 2 LITRES/QUARTS

Preheat the oven to 190°C (375°F) Gas 5. Lay the celery, fennel, carrots, onions and tomatoes on a baking sheet. Drizzle with the olive oil and place in the preheated oven for 45 minutes until the vegetables are well charred and very soft.

Transfer the vegetables to a large stock pot. Then place the empty roasting pan over medium heat and add the wine. Scrape up all the crispy and blackened bits from the bottom and then pour the contents into the stock pot.

Add the water, beans, herbs, dried mushrooms, peppercorns and salt to the pan and place over high heat. Bring to the boil and simmer for 1½–2 hours. The stock should be reduced to less than half the original quantity. Remove from the heat and strain the reduced stock through a fine sieve/strainer. Set aside to cool.

MISO GRAVY

This versatile gravy is packed with umami, the deep savoury taste often found in meat-based gravy. The sauce makes a great accompaniment to a traditional vegan roast dinner such as savoy-wrapped quinoa roast (see page 92). It can also be simply poured over roasted vegetables. The gravy will keep for 3–4 days in the fridge and can be reheated as needed.

60 ml/4 tablespoons olive oil or 60 g/2 oz. vegan margarine

1 tablespoon plain/all-purpose flour

1 litre/4½ cups roasted vegetable stock (see left)

1 tablespoon miso or soy bean paste

½–1 teaspoon salt, to taste

MAKES 1 LITRE/QUART

Heat the oil or margarine in a medium pan or frying pan/skillet, then add the flour and mix together to make a paste.

Cook gently over low-medium heat for about 1–2 minutes, then start adding the vegetable stock a little at a time. Mix well to ensure all the lumps have dissolved. Keep adding the stock (using a whisk can be easier at this stage). Bring to a simmer, mixing well to ensure a smooth, thick gravy.

Add miso or soy bean paste and salt and stir well. Taste the gravy and add a little more salt if needed.

INDEX

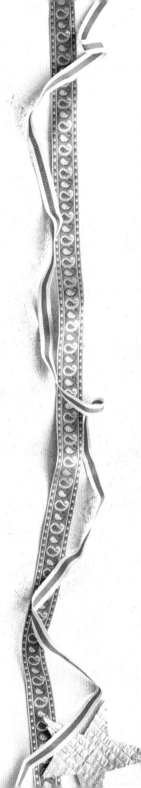

ACKNOWLEDGEMENTS

This book houses so many recipes that are often on the table for my own family celebrations and get-togethers. Sometimes food differences can be divisive but I very much hope that these recipes go some way to making everybody's holiday feasts more shareable. I'm very grateful to my own family and friends who've been open-minded about trying new things and broadening their own plant-based eating. I'm especially grateful to my good friend Charlotte O'Toole who shares so many great ideas with me, and helps me grow and shape delicious recipes.

I'm hugely thankful to our creative team who never fail to bring their A game, especially the shoot squad Clare Winfield, Megan Smith, Katie Gilhooly and Georgie Hodgson. And an extra special mention for Tony Hutchinson, whose infectious love of all things Christmas even managed to soften my Grinch-y-ness. Big thanks as ever to the RPS team, Miriam Catley, Leslie Harrington, Julia Charles, Cindy Richards and Mai-ling Collyer.

Thanks also to Agent Holly (Arnold), Lee James, Natalie Bissmire, Francesca Raphael, Natalie Coleman, Anne-Marie Goodfellow, Karen Bolan, Ping Coombes, Marianne Pownall, Lisa Messina, Amir Poran and all my friends who've helped me keep going in one way or another during the last year.

The publishers would like to thank Blackout Shop in Brighton and RE in Corbridge www.re-foundobjects.com for loaning decorations for the photography.